Patriotism, Peace, and Vietnam:
A Memoir

**by
Peggy Hanna**

**Left to Write
Springfield, Ohio**

Copyright © 2003 by Left to Write

Library of Congress Control Number: 2003106866

ISBN 0-9741865-0-3

*To all Vietnam veterans, their
families, and all who work for peace.*

Table of Contents

Foreword ix
Chapter One   The Move   1
Chapter Two   Hawk to Dove   7
Chapter Three   Springfield People for Peace   21
Chapter Four   Patriotism   30
Chapter Five   Witness   35
Chapter Six   Kent State and More   41
Chapter Seven   Mrs. Smith Goes to Washington   50
Chapter Eight   Opportunity Knocks   56
Chapter Nine   The Paris Peace Talks   60
Chapter Ten   Sharing the Experience   78
Chapter Eleven   Banned   82
Chapter Twelve   Pressing On   85
Chapter Thirteen   Peace to Politics   95
Chapter Fourteen   Political Realities   104
Chapter Fifteen   The End   107
Appendix   Brief Overview of the Events Leading to the Vietnam War   113
Bibliography   116

Acknowledgments

My deepest appreciation to my husband, Jim, for standing with me, encouraging me, and putting up with me.

I'm forever indebted to my peace friends—Ruth Rudawski, Karen Duncan, Jean Martensen, and Janet Baer—for their continual help and encouragement. To my writer's group, Linda Seibert, Matthew Gunter, and Vivian Blevins, I have to say "You're awesome! I couldn't have done it without you." And on behalf of our writers' group, I'd like to recognize McDonald's Restaurant in Troy, Ohio, for their hospitality.

Thanks to all who have read and critiqued this book, especially my dear friend, Chris Kelly Gunderman; my cousins, Bill McGivern and Helen Morrissey; and John Abma who's always there for me. Maddi Breslin's behind-the-scenes assistance gave me the boost I needed most.

Thanks to Donna MacMeans of the Central Ohio Fiction Writers group, Nancy Fischer and the other writers at the Memoir Intensive at the Antioch Writers' Workshop, Kathy Morrissey Thomsen who understood why I wrote this book, and the reference librarians at Clark County Library in Springfield, Ohio.

Finally, I want to acknowledge a special friend, Marion Balliet, who passed away in 1999. Marion served as Springfield People for Peace's one and only treasurer. Throughout her life, Marion personified the gift of peace.

Foreword

I was a peace activist during the Vietnam War. Identifying myself as one of those who protested the war, I fear some may not read any further; too angry or too bitter toward people like me. But please give me a chance to speak, to hear me, to know how much I cared about those who answered our country's call to serve and to fight.

I, a conservative Midwestern Catholic homemaker, mother of five small children, converted from hawk to dove in the late 1960s. Hawk or dove, I ached for all the young men suffering and dying because our country demanded it of them. My ache became anger as I learned more about our government and the politicians who created this horrible situation. My anger became activism, fueled by the knowledge that our young men, not the politicians or their sons, were paying the price for our leaders' stupidity. I was protesting government policy, not our servicemen and-women.

I cannot speak for a whole movement, but I can speak for our local peace group, Springfield People for Peace. We cared deeply about those sent to Vietnam, and I know countless others throughout this country did as we did—protested the war with only the best in our hearts for those dug in the trenches in Vietnam.

We respected those answering our country's call. Even though we believed the war to be wrong, it did not negate their sacrifice, their honor. We were with those men and women in spirit, aware how easy it was for us to be protesting compared to what they were living. But it was the best we could do.

Chapter One

The Move

1961—Newly elected President John F. Kennedy continues aid to South Vietnam.

1963—16,000 American military personnel in South Vietnam, up from Eisenhower's 900 advisors. Kennedy assassinated. Vice President Johnson becomes president.

1964—Tonkin Gulf Resolution opens door to war. Johnson says, "Our response . . . will be limited. . . . We seek no wider war." Johnson wins presidential election as peace candidate. By the end of 1964, United States has about 23,000 military personnel in South Vietnam, serving in a full but undeclared war, with fighting also in Laos and Cambodia. American casualties for the year total 1,278.

1965—Communist Vietnamese troops attack American military camp killing 8 Americans and wounding 109. Johnson responds with Operation "Rolling Thunder" bombing raids on North Vietnam through 1968. U.S. military personnel in South Vietnam rises to 184,300 by 1965. Americans killed in action for the year number 1,369 with 5,300 wounded. Republic of Vietnam Armed Forces (South Vietnam) killed in action for 1965 was 11,242.

March 1966—I had little knowledge of Vietnam. I knew we were sending advisors, and then ground troops, but didn't give it much thought. Even if I had, I would never have dreamed of questioning government policy. I'd been schooled by Catholic nuns all through elementary and high school: follow the rules; respect authority; don't ask why. The only precursor to my challenging American policy in Vietnam in 1969 was July 17, 1962, the day my first son was born. At twenty years of age, it was the first time I had questioned or challenged *anything*.

I'd been in labor eighteen hours. My contractions were eight minutes apart when my husband Jim and I decided to head to the hospital. It was an uncomfortable thirty-minute drive from our home in Griffith to St. Mary Mercy Hospital in Gary, Indiana. I especially remember the three sets of railroad tracks. Jim didn't slow down for any of them; he was in a hurry.

"Stop here," I said to Jim when I spotted the front entrance of St. Mary Mercy. What did I care that we were on a residential street and every parallel parking space was taken. Young and dumb, we didn't know to use the emergency room entrance.

"Let me out," I said confidently. "You can find a place to park." Always agreeable, Jim helped me out of the car, then left me alone on the sidewalk. Standing there, I looked up at what seemed like a thousand steps to the front door and hesitated. Wait for Jim or go for it? Knowing another contraction was due, I held the sides of my protuberance and headed up the steps alone. It was a sweltering July afternoon, ninety-something with no breeze. Sweating in maternity slacks and top, I grabbed the railing and dragged my swollen body up the steps, resting once for a contraction. Finally I made it to the top landing. That's when I saw the sign on the main door:

"WOMEN NOT ALLOWED IN SLACKS OR SHORTS."

My knees buckled. My heart sank. I had to go home to change my clothes! Tears welled in my eyes as I turned from the door and started down the stairs, holding tightly to the railing with sweaty hands. More than halfway down the monstrous steps, I experienced—not a contraction—but my first challenge to authority. I was having a baby! I was not going all the way home, over those railroad tracks, just to change my clothes. At that moment, Jim bounded up the steps to my side. In tears and with a rush of words and emotion resembling Stan Laurel of the Laurel and Hardy comedy team, I whined and pointed to the hated sign. "The sign says I have to go home and change my clothes but it's too far and I'm having a baby and I don't want to change and I'm not going to! I don't care what they say!" I expected an argument from him, but, of course, there was none. When we burst through the doors into a darkened lobby, a couple of women wearing employee nametags looked surprised to see us. I braced myself for the fight, but instead they rushed over with a wheelchair. No one said a word about my slacks. I had challenged authority, and it wasn't a sin.

I never challenged authority again until we moved to Ohio three years later. There in a little village named Yellow Springs, I came to believe it was a sin, in some circumstances, *not* to challenge authority.

* * * * *

In March of 1966, we rented a tired old farmhouse about five miles outside of Yellow Springs. Jim had been transferred, promoted from home office training in Joliet, Illinois, to a middle-management loan officer position in Springfield, Ohio. He had come home from work one evening and told me he was starting his new job the next day. In those days, there was no discussion about such matters. The *Company* had spoken.

Springfield, a declining mid-size industrial city of 80,000, sat in the midst of an agricultural county. Rentals in Springfield were scarce, especially for families with three small children. After a few lonely weeks, Jim found a white frame farmhouse in the center of 150 beautiful acres of pasture, woods, flat land, and rolling hills. It was about twelve miles from his office in Springfield.

He called to tell me about it. "I can't find anything that's even close to decent. Everything else is a hole."

"But a farm?" I imagined us as Ma and Pa Kettle, but quickly responded, "What choice do we have? Go ahead and take it."

Though I had never stepped foot on a farm before, I had always wondered what it would be like to live on one. When I was in high school, I knew of one classmate who lived on a farm. I used to stare at her in wonder trying to imagine what her life would be like—all that space, cows, pigs, horses, and no next-door neighbors. That was as close as I'd ever been to farm life.

When we told our families our decision, everyone thought it a huge mistake because they couldn't see me so isolated. I was a big city girl, raised in Chicago and its suburbs. "You won't last a month stuck in the middle of nowhere. You'll go crazy and then you'll have to move again!" my mother-in-law predicted. Her prediction ensured I'd try real hard to adjust. I wouldn't want to prove her right.

The morning after we moved in, we questioned the farmer, our landlord, about the nearest shopping area and closest Catholic church. An old guy in dirty over-worn bibs, leaning on a rickety fence that couldn't possibly keep all those cows out of our front yard, he told us Yellow Springs was the nearest town, a few miles away.

"But Yellow Springs ain't a place for you all," the old farmer warned us. "Go to Springfield. It's a lot bigger. More stores. Only ten miles as the crow flies."

It struck me a bit odd, his steering us away from the closest town.

"Why go further when that little town is so close?" I asked.

Crisscrossing lines etched his weathered face, his frown deepened them. He shook his head and pursed his lips. His eye twitched a little, then slowly drawled, "People, people like you, just wouldn't want to be around there. They've had some trouble."

"What kind of trouble?"

"Riots."

"Riots?"

"Colored man wanted his hair cut and that barber weren't gonna cut no nigger's hair. Them students got all worked up over nothin'."

My stomach knotted. Although I hadn't paid much attention to the civil rights movement, my dad had taught me the racial slur he used was worse than a cuss word.

The farmer continued, "Was a while back. But they got black and white mixing together if you know what I mean. Everyone goes to Springfield."

We thanked him for the information. Without saying anything to each other, Jim and I set out for the closest town, Yellow Springs. That's what you did when you had three little ones three years and under.

A little past noon, with two toddlers in hand and a baby in the stroller, my husband and I, our mouths gaping, eyes widening, stared at dozens of college-age students. Men and women both with long hair drooping past their shoulders, clad in multicolored shirts, and loose, long-flowing skirts or pants, jaywalked freely in bare feet or sandals, with a confidence that told us this, Yellow Springs, was their town. Jim and I had never heard of "hippies." That's what they were; only we didn't know it then. We only knew of the beatniks of the fifties.

After the initial shock of seeing our first hippies, we discovered the town to be quite a cultural challenge; not Chicago and not quite Mayberry. Old wooden storefronts leaking wafts of incense onto the sidewalk lined the street along with a mom-and-pop grocery (what strange-looking herbs and vegetables!), a hardware store, and a bank. Wind chimes tinkled and all manner of peace symbols, candles, organic foods, books, avant-garde art, and gifts crowded the windows.

Jim and I found ourselves on that street as though standing on another planet, unaware that the simple decision to go to the closest town would change our lives forever. This picture of us, befuddled and unknowing, symbolizes my painful yet positive transition from conservative Catholic hawk to peace activist. Only in hindsight would I know what that moment would always represent to me.

Chapter Two

Hawk to Dove

1968—The National Front for Liberation of South Vietnam (known as the N.L.F. or Vietcong) and North Vietnamese troops attack South Vietnam cities in the Tet Offensive. Between 1965 and 1968, 30,343 American troops killed in action; 14,314 in 1968 itself. The cost of the war is approximately $30 billion. President Johnson withdraws from the presidential race. Johnson calls a halt to the bombing and begins negotiations with North Vietnam. American troops in South Vietnam number 536,000. Rev. Martin Luther King, Jr., and Bobby Kennedy are both assassinated.

Country life immediately captivated me. Growing up on Chicago's north side, my childhood had been spent in an apartment building where we weren't even allowed to play in the small concrete backyard. For fun, my brothers and I climbed billboards that rose above the grit of Lawrence and Damen avenues. Not my sons.

Although they were still too young to do the things I dreamed for them, I learned how to milk cows and drive a tractor. The oldest helped herd renegade cows and ponies out of our front yard whenever someone forgot to close the gate. The scariest thing any of us faced was stepping in cow pies in the driveway outside the fence to our yard. Whenever we came home at night, Jim and I would carry the boys and tread lightly in the pitch dark praying with each step as if the cow pies were land mines.

That first summer, my youngest sister, Mary Ellen, sixteen years old and into drugs, moved in with us. My parents, fed up with her, thought we could straighten her out. We didn't have much hope for straightening her out but welcomed her. She was my little baby sister, and I loved her very much. Jim had always been partial to her too.

Through her, we learned more of the counterculture of the sixties than we would have otherwise. Once she brought home a flower child (not to be confused with hippie) whom she met in Yellow Springs. A very gentle, kind, young man, dressed in a loose-fitting, flowered-gauze shirt, he and Mary Ellen could have passed for twins with their slight builds, long blonde hair, and unisex clothes. He was a sixteen-year-old runaway. Coincidently he lived in Joliet, Illinois, our old hometown and belonged to our old church. I convinced him to let me call the priest to let his parents know he was safe. Eventually he did go home.

In spite of the farmer's warnings about Yellow Springs, we joined St. Paul's Catholic Church there. Our former church in Joliet had been the Archdiocese's Cathedral parish, huge, formal, and complete with a bishop. St. Paul's was more a little mission church. Jim would be happy at any church, but I seemed to be searching more for a place where I felt I knew people, and they knew me—like the sitcom of the '80s, *Cheers,* where everybody knew every body's name. Maybe in this small church, I'd feel I belonged.

That September the parish priest asked me if I would please help by teaching a religion class for sixth graders. Because there was no local Catholic school, all the parish children were to attend what was then called CCD (Confraternity of Christian Doctrine) religion class. The priest assured me I could handle it—just read from the book. He was so impressed that I had twelve years of Catholic education that I couldn't turn him down. I accepted my first volunteer job.

Through my new friends at church, I learned about the local college, Antioch, and the students who had caught our attention that first day. They were among the first hippies anywhere. The hippie movement was flourishing in the mid-sixties in California and in Yellow Springs, Ohio, but hadn't yet spread throughout the country. To some, Antioch College, a small, private, liberal arts school, was just ahead of its time. To others, it was communistic. Regardless of anyone's feelings about the college and its students, no one could deny its role in shaking people out of their apathy.

Yellow Springs' people were proud of their diversity and tolerance, but many outside Yellow Springs were intolerant and hostile to this community of intellectuals and "troublemakers." Country folk from surrounding areas would lock their car doors when driving through Yellow Springs.

One weekend my other sister and her family came from Chicago for a visit. Anxious to show them the sights (mostly hippies), we drove down the main street of town and around the campus. "Chicago doesn't have anything like this," I bragged.

"My God, look at them!" my sister cried out in shock as a half-dozen hippies crossed right in front of our car. One longhaired young man turned and flipped us off. We deserved it, I thought, suddenly embarrassed by our gawking as though in a zoo. Sightseeing wasn't uncommon though. Traffic often slowed on Xenia Street as tourists stared at the outlandish hippies and the colorful downtown.

One of my first friends at church was another volunteer teacher, Irene Kraus. She also had three young sons, and we instantly forged an alliance. Through her friendship, my life started its new journey. Irene's husband, Mike, a young history professor at Antioch, vehemently opposed the Vietnam War. I unquestioningly supported it. I was a patriotic hawk believing we had to do whatever it took to save that poor country from communism.

As I got to know Mike and Irene better, we talked and argued about the war. Though intimidated by Mike in his role as professor and by all the highly educated people surrounding me now (I never knew a professional or college-educated adult as a child and was in awe of these people who seemed to accept me), I valiantly argued against Communism and for the freedom of the Vietnamese people.

My father, first-generation Irish, who never needed to kiss the Blarney Stone for the gift of gab, used to argue with me, taking a devil's advocate position on most any issue just to provoke me. Just as I always lost to my father, I couldn't hold my own against a history professor. Forced to strengthen my position of supporting our government, I started to study about the war. Over time, I became more and more unsure of what I was saying (or parroting): the government's line. I had begun to question.

A bit paranoid, I worried that my new friends might be communists trying to brainwash me. What if Mike and Irene were communists, and I was too weak to stand up to them? The expression "a communist under every bed" was taking on a personal meaning.

Back in elementary school, numerous priests and POWs from World War II came to our class and told us the horrors of torture, imprisonment, and communism. Duck and Cover (the civil defense drill practiced in school where we ducked under our desks for protection from an atomic bomb) was our reality in the late 1940s and early 1950s. Communism was the devil. I loved our country and the freedoms we so proudly won. We were the good guys. I had to be strong and not let Mike and Irene undermine my faith in our country.

Then in 1967, even though he was classified as 3-A (head of family) and not subject to the draft, Irene's husband, Mike, turned in his draft card to protest the war. Of course, this meant he could go to jail. I didn't understand his taking such drastic action no matter what he believed. How could he risk jail when he had a family to care for? But Irene supported him, saying she understood because she had grown up in Lithuania during World War II. She knew what war was. She told me about being hit by an American jeep when she was only six years old. Maybe she was just prejudiced!

By law, all eighteen-year-old males had to register with their local selective service board and carry their draft card with them at all times. While some protesters burned their cards, Mike purposely chose to turn his in to underscore his protest of the war and the draft itself. His draft board immediately reclassified him from 3-A (head of family) to 1-A (delinquent) a punitive step that meant he'd be drafted immediately. He refused induction, and his case, along with so many others, headed to the courts. Not understanding the process, I feared he'd be sent to jail immediately. I couldn't imagine how I'd survive if my husband had done something so reckless. I admired Irene for her strength. But luckily the courts would take time, and Mike's family didn't pay the price for his political statement.

During these years 1966 to 1969, I grappled not only with the question of Vietnam but with the changing Catholic church, civil rights, and the women's movement. The influences of my new environment and friends chipped away at every foundation of my life. Life had been so predictable during my teenage years, the 1950s. I wanted to be like Donna Reed, TV's quintessential housewife and mother on the *Donna Reed Show*. My family life as a child was far from *Ozzie and Harriet,* but that's what I dreamed of for my children.

My earliest childhood memories are of me, my two brothers, and sister, sitting on the steps of various taverns in Chicago's north side waiting for our parents. They lingered inside, apparently not worried about us, for what seemed to me to be hours. They should have been worried because I remember one time a man came out of the tavern and offered us candy to go with him in his car. My older brother wouldn't let us go with him.

My youngest sister wasn't born until 1950 after we moved to a western suburb. It was a "dry" town, meaning no liquor could be sold. On the day of our move, my dad discovered the hardware store where drinks were sold in the back room. The family euphemism became "Dad's at the hardware store."

My father was a dining car steward for the New York Central Railroad. He often met famous people on his run on the *20th Century Limited* from Chicago to New York.

Among them, he met the parents of the five Sullivan brothers who died in a navy battle in the Solomon Islands in 1942. He was especially proud to tell people that particular story; how nice the parents were, how brave, how much they must have suffered. When I was thirteen or so, I saw the movie, *The Fighting Sullivan's,* which followed the five brothers as they grew up (very Catholic) through their enlistment into the navy right after Pearl Harbor and to their deaths. I cried and grieved as though I had known them. (A precursor of the grief I felt during Vietnam?)

Dad would be gone to New York for five days and then home for a few days until his next trip. At home, he was always drunk. In the early fifties when I was in sixth grade, I remember looking in the mirror in my bedroom, watching the tears creep down my cheeks after another disastrous dinnertime. "He's drunk. He's mean because he's drunk," I cried out loud. I didn't know the word alcoholic, but even at that moment of recognition, I knew my dad loved me, and I loved him. Lots of children of alcoholics never knew they were loved, but I did.

An extremely intelligent and well-read man, with an almost photographic memory, my dad loved to debate and argue any subject. I'd always end up in tears, not because I was unable to match wits with him (after all I was only a kid) but because of his sharp Irish tongue that made me feel inadequate and humiliated. However, at other times, he'd show he had confidence in me by challenging me to become a jockey or a sports reporter, careers unknown to women back in the mid-fifties. Of course, I thought he was crazy. I wanted to be a wife, mother, and secretary.

The jockey career was a favorite because he loved to play the horses, and I was small. He used to take me to Arlington Park Racetrack where he taught me how to read a racing form. I was in first grade then and felt extremely proud that I could read a form when I knew lots of adults couldn't.

Unlike most families during the mid-fifties, my mother worked. She got a job at Illinois Bell as an information operator when I started the sixth grade. My dad had fallen and broke his leg (yes, he was drunk), and she had to work to make ends meet. It was supposed to be temporary, but she never quit.

My guess now is that as a child living in an alcoholic home (my mother also drank) where there was no consistency in rules or structure, I grounded myself by latching onto the authority of the church and society. I needed the security of a respectable and responsible authority. Then with our move to Ohio and the shifting times, suddenly my foundations, my security were shaken. I wasn't alone, of course. The sixties hit everyone.

* * * * *

Through those few years 1965 through 1969, I vacillated between feeling challenged, attacked, and nurtured on four fronts: the war, the church, the women's movement, and civil rights.

I had never thought of the Catholic church needing to change. I didn't understand when Pope John XXIII called The Vatican II Council (1962–65) to "open a window." (Now I think that open window had a screen on it.) But with faith, hope, and optimism, in 1967, Jim and I joined a study group from St. Paul's to prepare for the changing church, and I learned to open my mind. I began to question. Was there anything that was intrinsically evil? Abortion? Why couldn't women be priests? Why couldn't priests marry? What about the population explosion and birth control? I began to hope for changes that would never be. In 1968, Pope Paul VI issued his encyclical on birth control and stayed the course: Birth control was still a sin. That was one issue that hit home! I was getting rather nervous about my potential for having twenty kids. Jim, on the other hand, didn't concern himself about it. God would provide.

And the war raged on.

The women's movement challenged my traditional and unquestioning role of wife. Jim liked me the way I was before the women's movement. He was in control.

Luckily, he listened as I recounted stories of stereotyping and injustice, stories I heard from educated women whom I respected and admired—women who aspired to be more than a wife, mother and secretary. Even so I drew the line at the question of flying in a commercial airplane piloted by a woman. Equal pay for equal work sounded right. But a woman pilot? It took many more years before I fully appreciated the movement and, yes, would welcome a female pilot. Jim said he was grateful I wasn't burning my bra.

Ours had been a romance born in darkness. We met in a broom closet. I was fifteen and he seventeen when his friend pushed both of us into the broom closet at a party. Flattened against each other, in total darkness, his buddy held the door closed for more than a few minutes. Can't say it was love at first sight (because we couldn't see each other), but we planned our entire lives within three months of that first encounter. We'd get married in five years when he'd be a senior in college. It had to be a September wedding because he wouldn't graduate until June, and I'd be sure to get pregnant right away. (No birth control, no family planning other than planning to have a baby!) As it turned out, I didn't get pregnant that first month. I cried in disappointment. No more tears that second month though! Our first baby was born in mid-July.

After my high school graduation, I worked as a secretary in downtown Chicago and saved every cent I could. Jim inspected my savings book every payday to make sure we were on target. I thrived on his very positive praise when he saw the numbers growing. In spite of my dad, I never gave serious thought to going to college. I had the grades okay but no money and no real inclination that someone like me could go to college. However, I was committed to Jim's getting a degree. He needed a good job to take care of all the babies we might have.

In 1961, I had vowed to love, honor, and obey, but in the late sixties, I asked "Obey?" Well, two out of three was going to have to be enough.

And the war raged on.

Regarding civil rights, I hadn't paid much attention though I was conscious of racial discrimination and believed it unjust. It just hadn't touched me personally. I had once told a friend back in Joliet that I had no interest in coming with her to hear Martin Luther King. What did it have to do with me? Only in the late 1960s did I start to come face to face with my feelings about race. One incident underscored my mixed feelings of fear, racism, and empathy.

On April 6, 1968, two days after Dr. King's assassination, alone in my car, I was pulling out of the IGA parking lot south of Yellow Springs. Traffic was heavy on Route 68. As I waited at the stop sign for my chance to turn right, I noticed two average-looking, young black men hitchhiking about 100 feet from me. They looked right at me. Not past me, but at me. Remembering the morning headlines about racial violence across the country, I became uneasy and wished for a quick break in traffic. There was none. I kept a watchful eye to my left for my chance to pull out. Before I knew it, one young man was opening the front passenger door and the other was getting in the back seat. As they got in, the one next to me said, with authority, "We need a ride to town."

I didn't figure they'd listen if I just asked them to get out. Covering my fear with a cocky confidence, I asked, "Don't you think you should ask first?"

"Sure," one answered. Neither of them moved or said anything more. I had expected an explanation but got none. Downtown Yellow Springs was less than two miles away. *They could walk it,* I thought. But then with a break in the traffic, I turned onto the street and hoped for the best.

"Are you Antioch students?" I asked, thinking that would make me feel safer. But they said no. *Stay calm,* I told myself. *It's a short ride. . . .*

The one next to me said, "We're just comin' back from a memorial march," and then added as if I might not know, "for Dr. King."

Traffic moved slowly and my eyes never left the road. They wouldn't need to worry about my describing them to the police if it came to that. I got the feeling they thought I—or the world—owed them a ride.

But then they began to ask me questions, questions about my family and where I was from. *Imagine if they were white,* I told myself. *Would I still be so afraid? Hell, yes!* I thought. *No one has the right to just get into someone's car.* But these were special times, and Yellow Springs was a special place. I began to be unafraid.

"I'm really sorry about Dr. King." I offered my condolences but the words seemed so trite. "It's unbelievable that someone would do that."

"No, it's very believable. King knew it was coming. We all did," my front passenger said.

That hurt. They're right. Of course, it's believable. I looked straight ahead at the line of cars in front of me. *How can I let them know I'm on their side?*

"You're right," I said. I felt guilt and sadness. Never had I done anything about the civil rights movement. *I wish they could see they matter to me.* The ride suddenly became too short. *I didn't want them to write me off like any other white person.*

When we got to downtown Yellow Springs and its two-block strip of unique hippie-like storefronts, they told me to pull over. As they got out, they thanked me for the ride. *Sure, any time,* I thought to myself.

Like a rapid report of a gun, the church, the women's movement, and civil rights exploded around me at the same time as the Vietnam dilemma. However, my days weren't all that free to pursue serious study and reflections about any of them—except the war. Our fourth son had been born nine months after we moved to Ohio, in December 1966. I worked part-time for a Yellow Springs architect and babysat Irene's three little boys to bring in a little extra income. As much as I could, I listened and learned, grew and changed, a slow evolution I believe could only have happened in Yellow Springs.

* * * * *

Every possible weekday that I could, I listened to the Phil Donahue radio show, *Conversation Piece,* out of Dayton. I ironed more than ever, justifying my time glued to the radio. His Quaker (Religious Society of Friends) guests were the gentle souls who touched me. I began to trust Irene's husband, Mike Kraus. With much pain, I slowly came to grips with the fact that this time America wasn't "the good guy." The first time I heard that *my* America in its role in Vietnam was accused of actually violating several international treaties (the United Nations Charter, the Geneva Accord, and the SEATO Treaty), I didn't believe it, but it soon became obvious this was a known fact, one that our leaders apparently didn't think mattered. After almost three years, I finally came to terms with what our government was doing—and not doing. No moment of reckoning. Just a slow torturous evolution of mind and spirit.

Immersed in the "Just War Theory" (as taught for centuries by the Catholic church) in high school, I looked carefully at those tenets as a guide to the moral question of the war. I applied them to our role in Vietnam. A "just" war:

- must be fought for a just cause,
- all other ways of solving the problem must have been exhausted,
- there must be a serious prospect for success, and
- the use of arms must not be worse than the evil to be eliminated.

As I weighed what I learned about our situation in Vietnam against these principles, I became more disenchanted with our government and its policies. More angry. The history of Vietnam[1] was not disputed. We were indeed violating international treaties. I began to perceive the Vietnamese struggle for independence as akin to our own Revolutionary War. The conflict between North and South

---

[1] See Appendix for brief overview of the events leading to the Vietnam War.

Vietnam after the 1954 Geneva Accords was like our American Civil War. What if another country had fought alongside our South and declared us to be two separate countries with the North the aggressor against the South? Revolutionary war, civil war, just war . . .

Felix Green's book, *Vietnam! Vietnam!* (Fulton Publishing Company, 1966) with its amazing photos of women, children, Buddhists, and military touched me deeply. In his foreword, he wrote, "I am wholly certain that if the people of the United States only knew the background of the war in Vietnam, and what is being done there in their name, that they would insist on the war at once being brought to an end." Finally, I agreed. This was 1968.

No longer did our government's call, in the guise of patriotism, to fight communism and to remain strong in our quest to spread democracy and freedom touch my heart. The stories of the human costs, both to our service personnel and to the Vietnamese people, are what spoke to my heart. We were destroying the country and the people we were supposedly trying to save. We were killing our own sons or daughters or at best asking them to suffer untold physical, emotional, and spiritual harm. Why? To protect *our* democratic way, our freedom? No! We weren't even doing that. We, our country, our country's leaders, were simply saving face.

Through those years, I had struggled long and hard over who was telling the truth. What sources, media, people could I believe? I had worried whether Mike was a communist. What if all these smart college people were communist dupes? Now thirty years later, I know with no sense of satisfaction that the American people were duped.

In 1995 Robert McNamara, Secretary of Defense under President Johnson, confessed in his book, *In Retrospect: The Tragedy and Lessons of Vietnam,* that the Johnson administration was wrong, that Johnson knew the war was doomed, and that the American people were lied to. And in 1999, in his follow-up book, *Argument without End,* McNamara confirms not only that we were lied to, but our various administrations and leaders were unbelievably inept (my words, not his, but close enough) in their politics and policies. Only now do we, as a country, know just how badly we were deceived.

* * * * *

In September 1968, the farmer sold the farm. Expecting our fifth baby, Jim and I moved the family to Springfield. We had looked at a tract home on the south side of town. I remember the realtor cautioning us that we wouldn't want to move there (sound familiar?) because a lot of blacks were moving in, and "you know what that means." My consciousness had been raised enough in those past three years to know that an integrated neighborhood would be a good thing for our young family.

Me? I never knew any black people in my whole life. I remember an incident back in 1957 when two black teenagers, brothers, came to our church's monthly high school dance. The parent/chaperones made them stand at the door while hotly arguing about letting them in. Finally they were admitted. The next day, my entire English class debated the morality of barring the two boys. The bigger question then became: What would you do if one of them had asked you to dance? I wasn't sure what I would have done, but I felt the right thing, the Christian thing, would have been to accept the invitation.

My high school (enrollment 1,000), all girls, was almost all white. We had one black student. I didn't know her or have any classes with her, but most mornings I saw her get out of a limousine driven by a black chauffeur. I never knew whether he was her father or if she was wealthy. We all wore uniforms so it was hard to tell. For me, wearing uniforms was the great equalizer. I guess it was for her, too.

Jim's experience with other races was as negligible as mine. We didn't want our children to grow up as insulated (and ignorant) as we had been, so we ignored the realtor and purchased a split-level house in the integrated Southgate neighborhood. Cheaper housing helped our decision.

We were able to assume the previous owner's loan with no down payment—without the aid of a realtor.

No longer babysitting for Irene or working for the architect, I sold Amway soap products door to door or over the phone. It was the only job I could manage because I was pregnant again and had our four little boys at home.

Our move to Yellow Springs opened my mind. My move to Springfield would open doors.

Chapter Three

Springfield People for Peace

1968—Tet Offensive heightens popular doubt about war. President Johnson withdraws from the presidential race. Richard Nixon wins election.

1969—Nixon authorizes bombing of North Vietnam and, secretly, Cambodia. Antiwar sentiment continues to mount with dramatic demonstrations in the fall when news of the 1968 My Lai massacre breaks.

Away from the influences of Yellow Springs and preoccupied with our move to Springfield, I didn't pay much attention to the presidential election of 1968. I voted for Humphrey but with no excitement or conviction. Both Humphrey and Nixon campaigned on ending the war, but neither candidate gave any specifics on how he'd do it. How could I trust either of them?

Late summer of 1968, Jim and I packed up our four sons for a trip to visit both sets of grandparents back in the Chicago area. Dinnertime at my parents' home turned into a bout of indigestion. My younger brother, a self-avowed communist and atheist, had demonstrated at the recent Democratic National Convention in Chicago and witnessed the police brutality there. My older brother espoused an ultra-conservative line. The three of us with me as a fledgling peace advocate, argued intensely, each trying to persuade the rest of the family to our views. My dad did his best to keep us agitated.

On the other hand, dinner with Jim's family offered sanctuary for us, with lots of laughter, joking, and no war talk at all. The only bone of contention during our stay was our four little boys' Beetles-like hair cuts.

Back home in Springfield, a nun helping the various parishes with the CCD programs had introduced me, as she put it, to a "kindred soul," Ruth Rudawski. Although Ruth was fifteen years older than me, we connected immediately. We delighted in our mutual awakening to the realization that obedience was not to be blind.

Ruth, too, had been struggling about Vietnam. An attractive woman and mental health nurse, Ruth was the mother of four teenage daughters and a twenty-year-old son. Her son, Guy, had left home at age sixteen to become a brother in the religious order of the Marianists in Dayton. But four years later, he had given up on the religious life, rejoined the family, and thus, became eligible for the draft. Ruth feared she might have to give him up again, this time, in her words to an "inexplicably evil war."

The news of the My Lai Massacre, which actually took place a year earlier in March 1968, became public around the time our fifth baby was born. Colleen (finally a girl!) arrived in early April 1969. Our American troops had murdered hundreds of unarmed South Vietnamese civilians. I could barely comprehend that our soldiers could be so *inhuman,* but came to see it as a consequence of the military's *dehumanization* of the Vietnamese people—and of our own soldiers.

The irony of watching our men at war while America ate dinner in our comfortable homes didn't escape anybody. It wasn't the movies. It was real. The news photographers filmed live combat, risking their own lives as they covered the war. Reporters, soldiers, civilians—I couldn't believe anyone could experience such horror and survive. Repulsed by what I saw, I still stayed glued to the news reports. It was as if to *not watch* would be to deny the sacrifices our fighting forces were making. It would be the easy way out. I wouldn't pretend the war didn't exist, or that it didn't affect me. It did exist and it did affect me, and I would not be counted among Nixon's "Silent Majority."

In June, I spotted a brief article in the *Springfield Daily News* that mentioned a local peace group meeting, open to the public. I read that article over and over again. If I didn't do something then Nixon *could* count me as part of his silent majority. My freshman religion teacher used to repeat a quote to us that kept creeping back into my mind: "If you're not part of the solution, you're part of the problem." She was right.

Jim tried to understand my strong feelings, but still wasn't convinced our role in Vietnam was wrong. Looking back now, he says he felt then it was easier to just accept what the government had in mind for us. He was more concerned about the changes occurring in my life due to the women's movement and the church, knowing they'd have a significant impact on our marriage, an impact he feared. I wasn't aware then that he felt so threatened. Obviously, he also thought it was easier to simply go along with me, so he willingly watched the kids while I went to the meeting. The time had come for me to put my faith into action.

Once I had made up my mind, I called Ruth, and asked, "Will you go with me?"

"Sure," she said. "I can't just sit here and cry."

* * * * *

The meeting was held in a middle class neighborhood home, not far from Wittenberg University, a small liberal arts college in Springfield. Although much of that first meeting is but a blur now, some things I'll never forget.

I don't know exactly what we had expected, but these women (no men present) didn't look like hippies or students. They looked like us. Most of them appeared to be in their forties. There were about ten of them, and they welcomed us with a friendly and open spirit. Ruth and I sat on folding chairs pulled into the doorway between the dining and living rooms. Primarily faculty wives from Wittenberg University, the group was always open to "townies." Strong, educated, caring women, they gave us a bit of history about themselves and proudly talked of their accomplishments as a group. They had recently presented a petition calling for "Peace Now" to Congressman Clarence J. Brown, Jr. In only two days over Mother's Day weekend, they had collected 1,531 signatures.

A couple of the women had sons who were already stationed in Vietnam. One mother whose twenty-four-year-old son had returned from Vietnam over a year before said he never talked about the war at all, except to tell of the young kid-soldiers jumping from helicopters into the jungle. It was the young ones, the eighteen-year-olds, he had talked about. They were told not to walk on the jungle path. With a forty-pound pack on their backs and machetes in hand, they were to clear their own way because land mines booby trapped the paths. He said the young ones, the eighteen-year-olds who thought they were invincible, would just walk on the path and get blown up. None of us talked for several minutes. The images of these boys dying, their fear, their suffering, and that of their families—all caught up in a silent prayer—burned inside me. I had to do something, no matter how small or futile, to help stop this war.

Empathy welled in my heart as a white-haired woman talked about her son in Canada. "We knew the war was wrong and didn't want him to fight and die for something that made no sense," she explained. "If he'd wanted to go, that'd be his decision, but he didn't." She looked directly at me, and I nodded my head in sympathy. I didn't know what to say. Ruth's son would probably go if called, and he didn't believe in the war either. I was grateful my boys were too young to go through this.

Tall and stately, the white-haired woman sat down next to Ruth and me and searched our eyes for understanding. I wonder what quality of understanding my eyes reflected through the confusion I felt.

She continued talking. "He couldn't qualify as a conscientious objector." She laughed that resigned kind of laugh so laced with frustration. "We're Methodists," she said. It was widely believed that only long-standing members of pacifist churches such as the Quakers and Church of the Brethren could be exempted from military service as conscientious objectors.

One of the other women sitting across from us spoke up. "That's why draft counseling is so important," she said. "We're trying to show these kids what options they have." I didn't know much about draft counseling and was surprised to hear it was available in Springfield. Yellow Springs, of course, but Springfield? I had a lot to learn.

"I'm grateful he's safe, but we can't be in touch with him," the white-haired woman continued. She had everyone's attention now. "Our phone's tapped. We hear from him through his friends." Sympathetic heads shook in unison. "He may never be able to come home. He's had to leave everything, even his country. Because he thinks it's wrong to kill in a war that's nothing but lies." She paused, then added, "And he wasn't going to die for lies."

Ruth spoke up. "Guy, my son, may have to go and I'm sick about it," she said reaching for the other woman's hand. "I'll support him if he goes to Canada." Others nodded in agreement.

The woman lowered her eyes. I was sure she was fighting back tears. With her head still down, she said quietly, "I feel awful for those mothers whose sons will never come home from Vietnam. Given the choice, wouldn't they rather see their boys go to Canada?"

"No," an older woman across the room said. "For some people, guys who go to Canada are only one notch above deserters." I cringed at her harsh words but everyone seemed to agree.

"'My country, right or wrong,' or 'America: Love it or leave it,' that's what they say," she continued. "And they wave their flags of patriotism and send their sons off to be killed."

It was hard to hear it said that way, but I felt there was truth to her words. I knew if I hadn't moved to Yellow

Springs, I'd be like those mothers. After all, there are things more important than life itself. Things worth fighting and dying for—but what mother would want to send her son to Vietnam if she knew the real truth about the war and our role in it?

"I hate those slogans," I blurted out. "They make it so easy to look the other way. To never question." I laughed at myself, thinking what a long way I had come.

Treesa Liming, a soft-spoken woman in her mid-forties with long, dark hair pulled to the nape of her neck, stood up. With a quiet hand gesture, she signaled the discussion over, and called the meeting to order.

Later Treesa shared with me that she had been speaking out against the war privately for years, but then her own son had been drafted. He left for Vietnam, and Springfield People for Peace was born. Its other mothers were Lois Schrag and Louise Bindman. All three women were married to faculty members at Wittenberg University. Their first formal event was sponsorship of a group of students who were traveling throughout the country to speak out against the war. Later, when both the Schrags and Bindmans moved away from the area, Treesa and another faculty wife, Carolyn Swanger, took on the leadership of Springfield People for Peace. Marion Balliet, also a faculty wife, served as treasurer through the group's entire existence.

As Ruth and I listened, it became clear that at a previous meeting Treesa had let the group know she had to step down as leader. As dedicated as these women were, none felt they could step up and take the responsibility for leadership. Ruth and I were stunned. We wanted desperately to do something, to make a difference, to end the war. We didn't want this opportunity to disappear. We needed this group. We sat on the fringe of the women crowded into the living room. I looked at Ruth. She shook her head in disappointment.

Treesa was asking, begging, "Couldn't a couple of you take it on as co-chairs? We can't let it die."

The silent response made it apparent that no one was stepping forward.

"Ruth," I whispered. "Can we do it?" I knew without a question this group was what I had been looking for. I needed them. I couldn't continue watching the news describing the horrors of the war, listening to the body counts, and pretend it didn't affect me, even though I had no son there, no father or brother or even a friend. But still, I could feel what it would be like to have a loved one in Vietnam or to be someone who *had* to go there. A few years prior, I would have certainly waved my flag and never question why. I'd have been willing to fight for my country or send my sons to war but then I had always assumed our country was right. Now our country was wrong.

I'd always believed that God came first, before country, family, or self, and that all moral decisions were to flow from that simple, but sometimes difficult, belief. I believed strongly in our country and in the freedoms we enjoyed—to dissent, to speak out—freedoms won by the blood of wars before us.

My dad never served in the military, too young for World War I and too old for World War II. But I grew up with great respect for our servicemen and-women who sacrificed so much for our country and our beloved freedom. In the late fifties, my older brother served in the Marines, and my younger brother enlisted in the Army in the early sixties. He served in Germany.

During World War II, I was a very young child living in Chicago. I remember the wreaths hanging on the doors or windows, and the black ribbons sadly showing that a son or husband had been killed. I remember seeing all the soldiers and sailors in uniform and admiring them so.

Early one evening, after the war (I was around five), my dad took me and my two brothers to one of the beaches on Lake Michigan where they were staging a "mock" war. My dad took us behind some ropes where no one else stood so we could see better. The crowds were far from us. Soon planes started dive bombing, dropping bombs on the ships out on the lake. They were really blowing up! Fires lit up the black sky. I could see objects flying off the ships into the air. I know now they couldn't have been sailors, but it scared me then to think they were. Booms thundered everywhere. Then things started exploding all around where we stood. Land mines, my dad told me years later. No wonder no one else was around us. We kids cowered and cried but then it was over, and we walked away.

Now I couldn't walk away.

I was not a joiner and never had been. In high school, too many responsibilities at home kept me from participating in any extracurricular activities. As a young adult, I had no experience with any organization, except teaching CCD.

"Will you help me if I say yes?" I asked Ruth.

She nodded, and I raised my hand. Everyone fussed over us. No one questioned who we were or if we were capable. They were just glad to find someone who was willing to help. Talk about warm bodies!

My husband understandably questioned my sanity in taking over the leadership for a group that I barely knew, but he didn't question my ability. He had more confidence in me than I had in myself.

* * * * *

About this same time, I met a new neighbor, Karen Duncan. A 1967 Wittenberg University graduate, she still looked like a coed, with thick, long, black hair she always referred to as her bush. Her husband Ron, Wittenberg class of '66 football and basketball star, played professional football until he injured his knees and settled for a career in financial planning.

Almost five years younger than me with two boys the same ages as a couple of mine, Karen became an instant friend. Ours quickly became the kind of friendship where we talked every day, sometimes several times a day, about our kids and husbands. I loved Karen for how she reacted so emotionally to all my complaints. Whether it was Jim or the kids driving me crazy, she'd give just the right overreaction that'd make me laugh, and then I knew I could handle whatever the problem was. She always acted like she could never handle what I was describing.

The war found its way into our talk. Karen's husband wasn't in danger of being drafted and like many other Americans, she really hadn't come to a decision about our role in Vietnam. She had had no commitment to the cause of war nor to the cause of peace, but was beginning to question like I had, like so many Americans then. Karen wasn't sure about what she was hearing on the news anymore. Walter Cronkite, the popular CBS evening news anchor, was her hero, and he had proclaimed on national TV that he no longer believed the war was winnable. I invited her to join Ruth and me at our second Springfield People for Peace meeting. I knew she'd be open to what we could share with her.

"I'll come to hear what people have to say," she said. "Just for information." So Karen came with Ruth and me to our second meeting. Not surprisingly, when faced with all that we knew to be true, her commitment to oppose the war solidified. The three of us would never be the same. Our friendship would be forever.

Chapter Four

Patriotism

1969—Nixon begins to withdraw troops while turning war over to South Vietnamese. By year's end, U.S. military personnel in South Vietnam was reduced by 61,000.

Even though President Nixon announced the gradual withdrawal of American troops in June 1969, he continued the war by equipping the South Vietnamese to fight on their own. He called his plan the Vietnamization of the war. Although happy to hear about our forces returning home, my reaction to the news was basically negative for two reasons: First, I didn't trust Nixon; second, I didn't want our country to continue its hand in so much death and destruction. America was still part of the problem, not the solution. As the peace movement reacted to news of the president's "Vietnamization" plan, it quickly came to be seen as simply "changing the color of the corpses."

Horrific news reports at dinnertime continued to motivate me.

We, Springfield People for Peace, became a diverse group; mostly housewives and mothers, but men, too, professional people, blue collar, faculty, and students, even a couple of Vietnam vets. Two of our members' sons had already returned from Vietnam. Ruth's son was there. Guy had decided to volunteer rather than wait for the imminent draft call.

Ruth recalls:

> *He didn't want to hide away in Canada, even though I suggested and encouraged the idea. I realized that the years*

in the seminary had given him a strong sense of moral responsibility, and an idealistic notion of how the world works. It tore my heart out to watch him get on the plane and leave for basic training. A year later, I had to watch him board a plane again, this time it was for the unthinkable destination—Vietnam. My last words to him were "come back!" He promised he would but I was not appeased. As I watched him board the plane, it felt as though I was handing another innocent sacrificial lamb to a blood-thirsty and insatiable war machine, and all I could do was to stand there and scream inside. For the next twelve months, I cried each night until I finally fell asleep and had yet another nightmare. During the day, I kept judicially informed about the hideously frightening truth about the Vietnam War. It was, after all, on TV. I still anguish over the realization that this immoral war consumed almost 60,000 of our finest and most promising young men and women, our future.

One new member, Lou Ann Higgins, joined so other mothers might not lose their sons as she lost hers. I first met Lou Ann at one of our marches through downtown Springfield. She had read about the march in the newspaper and decided to join us. Someone had told me her son, Jerry, had been killed in Vietnam in November 1969, and suggested I ask her to lead the march. I hesitated, maybe afraid to open wounds, but decided to give her the chance to say yes or no. She didn't hesitate, saying simply, "I'd be proud to." One very brave woman, I thought.

Lou Ann, too, was raised Catholic. She once told me, "If somebody said something, then that's how it was." I knew exactly what she meant: We trusted, we believed, we followed. She had always wanted to get married, have children, and be the good Catholic mother. However, by the time her son Jerry was graduating from South High School in Springfield, she was convinced the war was wrong and did not want to see her son a part of it. Jerry, on the other hand, having been heavily recruited by the marines at his high school, was adamant he would join as soon as he graduated.

She even tried to entice him into college life by letting him take a Friday off from school so he could visit his older brother, David, at Kent State University. Lou Ann and David planned a great weekend to show off the fun side of college. On the way home, Jerry said to his mother, "Mom, I know what you're trying to do. You never let us miss school in our life and now all of a sudden you say, 'Jerry, just take the day off.' But, Mom, it didn't work. I'm going to go." Lou Ann talked to him about going to Canada, but he wouldn't hear of it. She wanted to save her son but couldn't. He went into the service immediately after graduation.

Once Jerry got to Vietnam, in every letter and every tape he sent home, he'd say, "Mom, don't let my brothers go. It's the worse mistake I ever made." This was of little consolation to Lou Ann that Jerry had come to see her side after she received word that he was killed in action.

* * * * *

Several of us put together a pamphlet, *Is Peace Patriotic?* We wrote the following for the first page:

> *When a situation, which at first seems justified, becomes endlessly destructive, demoralizing, and dehumanizing, it creates a crisis of the spirit. In a national political situation, it becomes the patriotic duty of every American to form a moral and ethical decision and to act accordingly.*

The second part contained "Facts to Consider About the Vietnam War." We included an historical outline going back to the French/Indochina War, and the cost of the war in terms of our American soldiers and our national budget. On the back page, we ran a statement about patriotism:

> *Patriotism means love of one's country. To love your country does not mean* blindly *accepting and supporting its policies. We, the people, have the right and duty to help form the policies our country adopts.*
>
> *We, the Springfield People for Peace, accept this responsibility and invite you to join us by exercising your*

right as a citizen to express nonviolent dissent to the war in Southeast Asia, and to begin now to effect a positive permanent peace.

We published our pamphlet in the *Springfield News-Sun* as a letter to the editor. Our premise on patriotism created a wave of controversy, and the local newspaper editor challenged us with the *Webster's New International Dictionary, Second Edition, Unabridged,* definition of a patriot: "One who loves his country and zealously supports its authority and interests." *Was I a patriot?* I loved my country, and I was supporting my country's best interests while recognizing its authority. Our country's interests would be best served by ending the war. I recognized its authority by lawfully exercising my constitutional right of free speech and the right to dissent. I reasoned I *was* a patriot!

It seems to me now this controversy over patriotism was and still is at the root of the anger and pain of many who experienced Vietnam. The anger erupts at the most unexpected times. Recently I was at a dinner reception, seated at a table for ten, white tablecloths, crystal, the whole works. I joked and talked with a man sitting next to me, a man white haired, about my age, and twice my size. We had never met before, and we both enjoyed sharing our interests and family stories. After about forty-five minutes, I mentioned I was writing this book. "What's it about?" he asked.

"About my experiences in the peace movement during Vietnam," I answered. I've had negative reactions to this before but was unprepared for his response. He slammed his fist on the table, shaking the dinnerware, and startling the other guests. He cussed me out in a loud voice, embarrassing everybody around us. I feared he'd have a heart attack, his face reddened so. I quickly learned he had served as a Navy fighter pilot in Vietnam and hated every one of us *"traitors."*

During the later years of the war, even when a majority of Americans opposed our role in Vietnam, much of that majority focused its anger and frustration on the peace movement. Public sentiment came to believe the war wrong or immoral or unwinnable, and at the same time resented antiwar demonstrators as unpatriotic. Demonstrators of draft age were branded cowards.

Today, many still believe peace activists were unpatriotic, even though we were right—and to be unpatriotic is to be un-American. A covert tension still exists nationally and within families. It may be hidden in most cases, but it's there. The peace movement remains a taboo subject among brothers and sisters, parents and adult children, friends and co-workers. We skirt around a piece of our lives, a part of our history, that caused immeasurable pain, physically and emotionally to those who served, those who protested, and those in between.

We who were involved in the antiwar movement were exercising the very freedoms so many service men and women have fought and died for. I couldn't understand how things got so twisted that those of us who took so seriously our duties as citizens and valued so highly our freedom to express ourselves could be seen as unpatriotic.

Chapter Five

Witness

1969—Over 9,000 American troops killed in action in 1969. American troops killed in action 1965 through 1969 totals 39,757.

Ruth and I, with the help of Karen and many others, grew in our leadership, and Springfield People for Peace grew in size and determination. As a group and as individuals, we affiliated with Another Mother for Peace, a national peace group based in California. Movie actress Joanne Woodward was one of their guiding mothers. We purchased their film, *You Don't Have to Buy War, Mrs. Smith* with Bess Myerson, former Miss America, as narrator. It was a powerful film about the "military industrial complex," the convergence of large corporate and military interests. President Eisenhower coined the term in his farewell address January 17, 1961. He warned, "We must guard against the acquisition of unwarranted influence, whether sought or unsought by the military industrial complex."

We offered the film as part of our continuing educational programs open to the public. Catholic Central High School in Springfield allowed us the use of the library or a classroom whenever we requested it. I simply called the principal, a nun whom I had never met, and she'd set us up in a classroom or the library. We also purchased and showed a very poignant film, *Another Family for Peace*. This was one family's story about a farmer, a World War II veteran, whose son was killed in Vietnam. He sat at his kitchen table, tears in his eyes. He couldn't understand how those fathers who had served in WWII and knew the horrors of war could willingly send their boys off to yet another war. And boys they were, on the average six years younger than the young men who fought in WWII. And for what? he asked.

Treesa Liming, our former chairperson, had put me in touch with Sig Goodman from the American Friends Service Committee (AFSC) in Dayton. AFSC originated in 1917 during WWII when a group of young Quakers refused to take part in the war and instead went to the battlefield to aid casualties of the war in France. Always disheveled though dressed in a suit (I think he only had one), Sig raced in and out of our meetings, pumping us up and sharing the latest information about the war and other peace actions. Then off he'd rush to another group in a neighboring county. His strength of purpose made me feel I couldn't let him down.

Springfield People for Peace believed strongly that we needed to stand publicly for peace in the hope that others might become convinced this war must end. So under Sig's inspired and enthusiastic guidance, we held weekly Peace Vigils on the sidewalk in front of the post office, the only federal building in Springfield. Anywhere from a dozen to twenty or so, we would stand in a single line, shoulder to shoulder, across the front of the building but not blocking anyone or any entrance, always peaceful and prayerful. Thirty minutes of silence and prayer.

I was always relieved when the time was up, and we could go home. The vigils were mostly my responsibility, and I prayed each time it would go as planned, nervously counting the minutes until it was over. No surprises, no violence. No time of quiet prayer for peace for me.

Occasionally to be more visible or in response to events in the war, we'd plan a march from the downtown esplanade to the post office. When it came to me marching, Jim, who managed a loan office in downtown Springfield, was concerned that my marching would cause negative fallout for his business.

"What's more important?" I'd ask. "Your business or ending the war?"

When we had been dating and first married, his mother had said I was like a puppy following him all the time. It was true—then. But in those few years after standing on that corner in Yellow Springs in 1966, the puppy matured into an adult (no, not a *bitch!*). Jim wrestled to understand my new consciousness as a woman and wife; my new independence. He struggled to balance his needs and fears against what he saw as my rights as a woman, not just as his wife. He never asked me not to march. If he had, what would I have done? To this day, I don't know.

Our marches were never spontaneous, like those on college campuses reacting to new and tragic turns in the war. We were too diverse to pull it off as quickly as they could. We planned ahead and let the police department know in advance. To their credit, they helped us by blocking traffic at intersections where we crossed, like a funeral procession. Our signs were homemade posters, and we chanted "All we are saying is give peace a chance."

Publicity for upcoming marches was nothing more than a notice in our newsletter and a brief press release to the newspaper. We were always thrilled to see sixty or more people attend. Springfield was a conservative, relatively small city with a dying downtown and a dwindling industrial base, like so many other cities then. It wasn't conducive to political activism.

I always checked with a local judge, sympathetic to our cause, to be sure we were on the right side of the law. His secretary would put my call straight through to him. It amazed me and made me feel important.

To my knowledge, no one in our group considered civil disobedience although a few of our members did withhold the telephone tax, a federal tax increased from 3 percent to 10 percent in 1966 to help pay for the war. After the war, the IRS audited one of them every year for nine years. Coincidental?

The others who had withheld their telephone tax were also audited. Just before one couple was to move out of the country in December of 1974, the IRS paid them a visit. The representative told them the IRS would get the money back one way or another before they left the country. She offered him lemonade and he mumbled something about someone having to do the job he was doing. His heart wasn't in it. It was some comfort to her. In the end, they did pay.

Our own membership was trained in peaceful and lawful demonstrations by Sig through the American Friends Service Committee, but both our vigils and marches were open to the public. That was the wild card. I was terrified someone from outside our own membership would break a law or somehow we'd inadvertently do so and be arrested. The jail frightened me but not as much as the prospect of being strip-searched, a nasty dehumanizing practice rumored common in such situations.

Some of our members worried that an FBI agent would infiltrate us and cause problems. Every now and then a bit of paranoia would strike and our discussions would be around "What if," "Who would it be," or "What would we do?" This was before Richard Nixon's Dirty Tricks of the 1972 campaign came to light, so we didn't really take it too seriously.

At both our vigils and marches, a few of us handed our pamphlets out to passersby. Some people were angry or disgusted with us, others embarrassed. Not a lot of eye contact. Occasionally someone would talk in support of the war, and we'd bend over backwards trying to stay calm and reasonable. It was difficult.

Never would we allow a piece of literature to be discarded and left as litter.

Sometimes we had our kids with us, partly because we didn't want to pay a baby sitter, but also because we wanted them to share in our efforts for peace. I remember my kids liked to carry the banner, "War Is Not Healthy for Children or Other Living Things."

Once our son, Kevin, who was about six at the time, said to me, "If the people next door to us are our neighbors and the people next to them are their neighbors and it goes on like that forever, then it means everybody is everybody's neighbor." Then he looked at me and asked, "Why would people kill their neighbors?"

Our largest march was Saturday, April 24, 1971, in conjunction with the Vietnam Veterans march on Washington. Over 150 people participated in Springfield. Again, police directed traffic. Several stores gave us permission to set up tables outside on the sidewalk to distribute literature and sign petitions to end the war. On legal grounds, we knew the sidewalks were public so we didn't need permission, but we asked so as not to be seen as disruptive.

One young demonstrator commented to a few of us as we marched, "Man, all the other marches I've been to, we just had the freaks. Here you have the middle age, middle class." We all laughed at his choice of words, but indeed were proud of who we were.

Bill McCuddy, the *Springfield News-Sun* photographer marched with us (off the clock). Working for the paper, he knew the FBI agents whose office was on the top floor of the post office building across the street from his. They had the habit of visiting editorial for pictures or information. Toward the end of the march, Bill spotted an FBI agent trying to fit in as a demonstrator. He wore an obnoxious fishing hat with beer labels all over it. Bill confronted him, "What the hell do you think you're doing here?" The agent ignored him and kept walking. Bill's wife, Melva, grabbed Bill's arm to keep him peaceful.

Twenty-four-year-old Bruce Dixon was a member of our group and the Vietnam Veterans Against the War. He marched with us, after returning from Washington that very morning. Two days earlier he had been arrested with other Vietnam vets on the steps of the Supreme Court building for failure to disperse. On Friday, Bruce joined other vets for a medals ceremony in which they threw their medals on the steps of the Capitol to protest the war. On Saturday, he was with us.

In a *Springfield News-Sun* article the next day, Bruce said his joining the Marines was a mistake due to "blind faith in my country" and he soon found out that the war was not to protect the freedom of the Vietnamese people. "I thought I was fighting for freedom, but it was just the opposite."

Because we were so "bland," we didn't rate the newspaper coverage the more exciting, violent, or disruptive demonstrations warranted all around the country. How many other groups marched peacefully but were known only to their own community? No one knows for sure, but I cannot believe we in Springfield, Ohio, were so unique.

The stereotyping of peace activists through the media—and through the military—caused undue pain to our servicemen and-women who believed we opposed them, and still do for the most part even today. We didn't. We supported them. We opposed our government's policies, not them! But they never knew the difference. How could they? They were fed horror stories of the antiwar movement while dug into trenches or crawling through jungles. I would have felt the same way. Maybe I am naive still, but I believe if our guys in the trenches had known people like us all over the country cared about them enough to turn our lives upside down to get them home, they would have felt some comfort. At least maybe they wouldn't hate us so.

Chapter Six

Kent State and More

1970—Nixon announces invasion of Cambodia. Kent State Shootings.

Irene, my friend back in Yellow Springs, and I had drifted apart as friends do when time and distance is put between them, but I was thrilled to learn her husband Mike didn't have to go to Vietnam or to jail. The Supreme Court struck down "punitive reclassification" by draft boards, meaning they could not reclassify a man just because he returned his draft card to protest the war. This is exactly what they had done with Mike. *Bucher et al v. Selective Service System,* on behalf of men who had been ordered to report for induction because they had returned their draft cards to protest the war, won their case in January 1970. This win gave me some hope at least for our judicial system. I had no hope for our executive branch.

Sometime in March 1970, we learned of secret bombings in Cambodia. Aside from a few rumors at the beginning, nothing was in the major media about it. However, the bombings were reported in alternative sources of the news such as the *American Friends Service Committee* and *Clergy and Laymen Concerned,* sources I learned to trust.

In response to the news about Cambodia, on a wintry March afternoon, a group of us mothers with our kids and handmade peace signs stood at the gate to Wright-Patterson Air Force Base. Our shoulders hunched up to brace ourselves against the freezing wind. Gusts of powdery snow blasted around in swirls on the concrete before disappearing. The kids kept asking, "How long are we going to be here?" Drivers leaving the base glared at us. One slowed down and a woman cried out, "You don't know how lucky and free you are." One of our group with her toddler on her hip responded, "We do know! And we value our freedom to dissent when our government is wrong."

My oldest son, eight-year-old Brian, noticed a white-haired, bearded man holding a blank sign. "Why doesn't his sign say anything?" he asked.

"I guess he thinks there's nothing more to say," I answered. I wasn't sure. Maybe the man was at a loss for words. Maybe he was crazy. Maybe we were all crazy. Did any of what we did really make a difference?

* * * * *

About a month later, on Thursday evening, April 30, 1970, on national television, President Nixon announced the U.S. invasion of Cambodia. He did not mention that we'd been bombing for a year. How could he not tell the country what had been happening for the past year? Could our information be wrong? (It wasn't. We know now, our information was correct.) Regardless, Nixon had campaigned on ending the war. He'd promised never to invade Cambodia, and now he was escalating the war. I was furious.

Through use of our telephone chain, Springfield People for Peace hurriedly organized a silent vigil for the next morning in front of the post office. Many of us, our kids in tow, then joined Wittenberg students on campus where 200 students and faculty stood in silence across from the student union. After a half hour of silence, people gathered on the grass to listen to speakers and commiserate.

The following morning, the newspaper's front-page coverage of the campus demonstration was overshadowed by an article about a random telephone survey conducted following the president's speech about Cambodia. The findings were indeed disheartening. In the Springfield area, 53 percent of the residents responding admitted they failed to listen to the nationally broadcast address on the increasing military action in Southeast Asia. One of the reasons cited was, "I don't pay any attention to politics or things like that." They chose to be blind to our national tragedy.

Demonstrations, the vast majority of which were peaceful, erupted across the country. Then on May 4, 1970, during an antiwar protest, four college students were killed by our own Ohio National Guard at Kent State University. It didn't seem possible that right here in Ohio such a tragedy could happen. It was the kind of headline you read about in other countries. I cried for the students, their families, and for our country. Where were we going?

Lou Ann Higgins, whose son Jerry was killed in Vietnam, had two other sons, David and Terry (Jerry's twin), both students at Kent State University. She panicked at the news of the shootings. David and Terry had to be safe. After a few hours of hell, her close friend, Melva McCuddy, who worked at the Springfield newspaper, was able to confirm that Lou Ann's two sons were alive, at least not listed among those killed.

David, just getting off work in the campus cafeteria, had walked out onto the hill where the shootings took place. He witnessed it all. Terry was off campus at the time and was frantic to get to his brother. When chided later about his going back to the campus that was sealed off, Terry responded, "Mom, my brother was there."

Less than a week later, Springfield People for Peace again joined the Wittenberg University students outside the student union and mourned the loss of life and the loss of innocence. Opposite to Antioch College in its image, Wittenberg—conservative, rich, mainstream—focused more on campus life than on Vietnam. While a small but committed student peace presence had been on campus, Kent State shocked the entire student body into action. It was comforting to me to be with so many students, peacefully and lawfully assembled, to express their sorrow and anger over Kent State. It didn't take any real insight to know this incident would further divide people and escalate the anger felt on both sides of the pro-government and antiwar factions and those still in the middle.

A couple days after Kent State, I returned to work in my job as ward secretary at Mercy Hospital. (In September 1969, I had taken a part-time job.) With no warning, a nurse, whose son served in the National Guard at Kent State, lashed out at me in front of the other staff.

"It's because of people like you that my son could have been killed!" she screamed at me. The only trigger for her outburst, I believe, was seeing me and knowing I was a peacenik—as though my being in the peace movement made me responsible for the situation at Kent State.

There was no way I could make her understand I was sick about it too. I couldn't defend myself. She was hurting too much, and I'd only make things worse. I wished someone else might speak up, but no one did. In fact, I don't remember anyone, in all the years I worked there, ever saying anything positive to me about my "extracurricular" activities. One nurse told other staff one evening that my kids would grow up to blow up buildings! Even the one conscientious objector who worked as an orderly kept his views quiet and didn't seek out mine. Because I worked mostly on the orthopedic and neurosurgery floor, we got to know each other pretty well, but when I'd tried to talk about the war, he'd change the subject. Between us, there was no talk about Vietnam. It was as if he just couldn't.

Some of our individual members supported the draft counseling efforts in Springfield but as a group we hadn't really been involved with it. They had a most difficult job. Clark County Draft Board 13A had been featured in an article in a national magazine as one of the most notorious in the country. Melva and Bill McCuddy's son, Jim, knew about the board's reputation and learned first hand how deserved this dubious distinction was.

Jim had been born with bi-lateral clubfeet. As a graduating senior in June 1970, he faced the draft. Even with the multiple surgeries he had, he knew he'd never survive combat because he couldn't run. In addition, he didn't want to serve because of his personal beliefs about the war itself.

His orthopedic surgeon gave Jim the necessary transcripts, Xrays, and letter verifying Jim was unfit to serve. With all the paperwork in hand, Jim and a friend went to the Clark County Draft Board office to register and begin the process of being declared 1Y, meaning he would be eligible for the draft only in the case of a declared war.

When Jim presented all his medical records to a woman at the office, she told him in a voice that reeked with contempt, "I'm not going to look at them. It's meaningless." She then threw all his paperwork into the wastebasket and added, "You'll go to Columbus for a physical—and you better hope you kissed your mama goodbye because if you pass the physical, you're not coming home."

Jim ended up enrolling in college and the following month, his father went to the draft board to request the proper form for the student deferment. Instead of handing the papers to Bill, the same woman with such contempt for anyone trying to avoid the draft, pitched them into the air. The forms scattered all over the floor. Bill, a decorated World War II veteran, was forced to crawl on his hands and knees in front of her to gather them up. The draft board's reputation, as not just mean but hateful, was confirmed.

Through the help of local draft counselors, Jim did protect himself and never went to Vietnam, but he still carries guilt for not going when so many others his age had to and were killed or injured. He told me he still asks himself, if he had been there, beside them, would it have made a difference? I ask myself if those politicians who cheered on the war feel guilt? They should, not Jim.

* * * * *

That summer of 1970 someone at one of our meetings suggested we sponsor a booth at the Clark County Fair. No one at the fair board questioned our application. Our peace booth, lodged between vacuum cleaner and insurance vendors in the Mercantile Building, was more visible than we had even hoped. No discrimination on the part of the fair board! We handmade various peace articles such as paper flowers, candle holders, macramé peace symbols, and burlap and felt wall hangings to cover the cost of the booth as well as raise funds for miscellaneous expenses. Another Mother for Peace medallions, posters, and stationery were hot items. I worried some about the possibility of hostile reaction to our booth, but there wasn't any. People mainly ignored us, but some quietly looked at our merchandise and/or literature. A few engaged in some debate, but I never heard anyone tell of being hassled. We invited people to join our group and a few did.

One day during the fair, Karen and I passed by the Clark County Democratic booth also in the Mercantile Building. A dark-haired, clean-shaven young man in slacks and dress shirt stood outside the booth, hawking for his candidate for state representative. We stopped to chat and within minutes recruited Vern Dunlap as our newest member of Springfield People for Peace. Vern, twenty-four years old, single, and an engineer, had recently moved back to Springfield. He'd been active in the peace movement in Erie, Pennsylvania, and was surprised and encouraged to learn of a local peace group. He came to our very next meeting. Like Karen, he immediately became an active member, and together they published our first newsletter (mimeographed, no computers then!). Vern's presence in our group, however, would have much broader implications. He was political!

Our membership grew to over 100 official members. Of this, probably ten to fifteen attended meetings regularly. Under Ruth's and my leadership, our programming focused on the Just War Theory. We were comfortable taking that approach with the churches that allowed us to make our presentation to adult Sunday school classes.

By now Ruth's worst fears had come to pass. Guy had decided to volunteer and not wait to be drafted. He tried to reassure his parents that he wanted to be a medic and minister to the wounded. He told them "War is an unpleasant fact of life, and I want to better understand it." They weren't reassured with his explanation.

Guy trained for the Green Berets Medic Division. Shortly after earning his beret, he tried unsuccessfully to get a weekend pass to come home for his sister's wedding. He was told he belonged to the corps now and the corp took precedent over everything else in his life. Uncharacteristically he defied authority and went AWOL, hitchhiked home, arriving in time for the wedding and leaving a few hours later to hitchhike back again.

Ruth remembers:

> *He looked so handsome and proud in his uniform and green beret. We didn't know he was AWOL until we learned about it in his next letter. He was caught, stripped of his hard-earned beret, reduced to a private, and sent immediately to Vietnam, another piece of "cannon fodder." It was about that time that my nightmares began, and the silent screams got louder.*

As an infantry platoon medic, Guy spent almost an entire year in continuous heavy combat on a firebase and in triple-canopy jungle. Wounded by shrapnel from a land mine, he spent two months in a hospital before returning to his unit. He was awarded the Bronze Star, a Presidential Unit Citation, the Air Medal, and the Purple Heart. He wrote in a letter that was published in the *Springfield News-Sun:*

> *I often ponder how a man's mind has the flexibility to survive the hideous confrontations experienced in this war. A safe speculation is that no man returns to the world, sanity intact.*
>
> *The monsoon rains are making a soldier's life miserable these days. Continuous, unceasing rains accompanied by freezing nights and various exotic skin diseases which never seem to heal. Vietnam is truly the "fun capital of the World."*
>
> *My experiences over here have allowed me a more clear insight into the mystery of life. The saying "you've*

never lived 'till you've almost died" is a frightening phrase and possesses a certain amount of truth. I fully realize that there is no glory in this war. Fighting for the freedom of oppressed people is a noble effort. Nevertheless, our country has blundered, squandering away many innocent youthful lives through involuntary servitude in this war. The right of the people to control the military must be regained along with peaceful coexistence.

His mother, Ruth, wrote the following in a letter to the editor: "I didn't always feel this way, tense and aching inside. At first it was only when I thought about the war. Now it's even when I laugh." She went on to say, "Today I got a letter from our son, a young man who loves his country, but, even more, he loves his fellow man. He wrote from a bunker in the steaming heat of the jungle of South Vietnam and described the war like this:

Each time death is in the air, or someone gets bummed up, you become a little more sick, sick at heart, and sick for home. I see these guys struggle and sweat all day and then wait in terror at night, not knowing when or from where, never knowing why. Even some of the lifers admit this war is wrong morally, regarding our involvement. I just wish people could always share and live together as well as the men in this platoon.

Ruth concluded, "Is there any decent American who doesn't ache inside?"

We all ached inside, but Ruth and those moms and dads whose sons were in Vietnam were overwhelmed. Ruth now believes she wouldn't have survived emotionally if she hadn't been involved in the peace movement. "It was an outlet for me. The members of the group, they were my support. It was literally driving me crazy to think what our country was really doing. Killing our sons, destroying a country and a people, pretending our cause was just. With the group, I didn't feel like a traitor but if I was alone, I would have been feeling very guilty about hating the war and feeling unpatriotic."

* * * * *

During those years, the early seventies, every evening in the comfort of my living room, I'd watch the national news and the devastating images of war and its toll on real people. Who could ever forget the picture of the young Vietnamese girl on a country road, arms outstretched as she screams in horror, her flesh burned off by our napalm. Watching the news reports from Vietnam reenergized me to do whatever I could to stop the bloodshed. Body counts, body bags. Men and boys being killed, being maimed. And for what? Nixon became the enemy for me, and I focused my anger on him. I had never been a political person, but that, too, was to change.

Chapter Seven

Mrs. Smith Goes to Washington

1970—Congress repeals Tonkin Gulf Resolution in June, an action Nixon disregards. U.S. troop strength in South Vietnam at end of 1970 is 334,600. Of them, 4,221 killed in action.

On May 1, 1970, Democratic Senator George McGovern and Republican Senator Mark Hatfield introduced the *McGovern-Hatfield Amendment to End the War.* They called for a stop to all funding for the war after December 1970 and the withdrawal of all American troops by June 30, 1971. A letter-writing campaign to our congressional representatives and senators in support of the amendment marked Springfield People for Peace's initial introduction to politics. Then that summer 1970 Ruth and I decided to go one step further. We'd go to Washington. We'd lobby our conservative Republican congressman to vote yes!

Ruth called and managed to get an appointment with our congressman, Clarence J. Brown, Jr., Republican, seventh District Ohio. Now we had to go. There was no turning back. We were excited at the prospect but apprehensive, too. Did we know enough to debate a congressman?

Jim gave his blessings as usual, staying home with the kids. Before I left, six-year-old Kevin got his ABC's and my peace activities a bit mixed up when he asked me, "When are you going to Washington, ABC?"

The American Friends Service Committee staff helped us by arranging for two college students on their way from

Cincinnati to DC to pick us up in Springfield. Neither of us wanted to drive the eight hours on our own so we gladly accepted the offer. Ruth and I crowded into the back seat of an old Volkswagen with the two young men in the front. Each had the long-haired, shaggy look and wore shirts and jeans that looked like they'd been on the road for weeks instead of hours. Ruth and I started out chatty, full of talk about the *Amendment to End the War* but soon realized they were polite but not big on conversation. We could only guess their feelings about our presence. Anything for the cause—including dragging two housewives to DC?

At one point, the driver asked for some coffee. Their thermos was hidden under a bunch of newspapers, bags of chips, and some old rags on the floor of the back seat. Ruth found it, poured some. As she handed it to the driver, the car lurched and the steaming coffee dumped on his shoulder. He screamed but luckily managed to keep control of the car. We hoped it wasn't an omen.

The two of us stayed at the Penn House, arranged again by the Friends (AFSC). I remember it was very late when we arrived. An elderly woman took us up the back steps to our room. The old wooden staircase lit only by the woman's candle gave me an eerie feeling. *Did Quakers shun batteries and flashlights? Didn't they have electricity?* It was like a throwback to some old-time movie. The stairs creaked, felt warped, and wobbled under our feet. The air smelled musty. I got to feeling very nervous about what we were getting ourselves into.

The woman showed us our room, which was large with two twin beds. We could join her and the others (what others?) for breakfast she told us and promptly backed out of the room with her candle. Yes, there was electricity: one 40-watt bulb. Ruth and I surveyed the room and started unpacking. I saw a door and thinking it a closet, tried to open it. After a couple of hard yanks, it opened. It took a moment for my eyes to adjust. I was standing at the side of a bed with a man in it! I remember almost doubling over to make myself invisible while I backed away closing the door very quietly. "Ruth! There's a man sleeping in there." With that, we fell into a giggling fit like a couple of junior high school girls.

The morning light changed the room to one of simplicity, practicality, and cleanliness. No bogeymen. When we joined the others for breakfast, a slight, older gentleman said he hoped he didn't scare us during the night when I had opened the door. Turned out he was a staff person with the Ohio American Friends Service Committee.

We joined them in their Quaker silent prayer in the living room. Ruth said she felt like she was among the apostles. They did have a special quality about them; peaceful, gentle.

After thirty minutes or so, I tapped Ruth on the shoulder, "Ruth, if we're walking there, we better get going or we'll be late." She shook herself out of her reverie, and we made our good-byes. We walked to the Capitol Building, agog at the sites and the hustle of important-looking people. We were on a mission though and steeled ourselves for the impending confrontation. We didn't have much hope of changing Congressman Brown's mind about his support of the war, but hoped we could infuse some doubt. Specifically, we would talk about the *McGovern-Hatfield Amendment*. Generally, we would plead for openness.

We were led into his private office where he sat behind a huge wooden desk and we sat in two small chairs opposite him. I felt like a first grader in the principal's office. No small talk like I would have expected. Tension filled the room. At first I felt unsure of myself, but then it became apparent Congressman Brown didn't even know the history of the war. He just spouted the traditional government lines. He reminded me of myself those few years earlier. (He didn't even feign "superior" knowledge of events like so many politicians did.) I knew more than he did, but it didn't matter. He wouldn't budge in his support of Nixon's war. I couldn't keep the tears back and felt naive and childlike as they flooded in front of him. For his part, he basically patted us on our heads and sent us on our way.

Ruth described the visit like this:

> *I felt like we were two refugees, humbling ourselves in the presence of this great image. I was in awe. I was still in the mode that congressmen and senators were our government. I had great respect for them. Not adoration, but awe for their office. That's how we are about the president even*

Patriotism, Peace, and Vietnam: A Memoir

> *if we hate him. This is the man who represented us even though we didn't vote for him. He was exactly what I thought he'd be. Pompous.*
>
> *I have no regrets at all. I loved every minute of it. Loved the idea of going into a congressman's office, eyeball to eyeball, even though he didn't hear what we said. He hadn't a clue as to whether he should take us seriously at all. Obviously he didn't. He didn't know anything about what we were talking about. We cried out of sheer frustration and the helplessness of it. This man doesn't know what we know and doesn't want to know. But he's making the decisions that keep the war going.*

After this very disappointing meeting, we toured the Capital Building, going anywhere we wanted with no one stopping us or questioning us. Ruth heard there was a tram between the Capital and the Senate building so we set out to find it. We found our way to the basement and wandered about for quite some time, before finding the train. I kept saying we had no right to be on it since we didn't work there. I was afraid we'd be thrown off, but Ruth kept saying we paid for it with our tax money. Again, nobody said anything to us.

We stopped at our Ohio senators' offices as well as several others and voiced our support of the amendment to their staffers. Somehow we never conveyed the urgency we felt, but we ended up getting a pass to the Senate chambers and watched the proceedings from the balcony, though hardly any senators were on the floor.

That evening as dusk drew closer to dark, we stood on a street corner trying to decide how best to spend our remaining hour before the students picked us up in their little VW for the dreaded trip back. We had been warned plenty of times not to be out on the streets after dark. While debating the pros and cons of each suggestion we came up with, I noticed a rough, disheveled-looking "bum" heading our way. *Oh, my God,* I thought. *We've got to get out of here.* We pretended to be engaged in conversation until he passed. Relieved, I watched him cross the street. Then all of a sudden, he turned and headed back toward us. I grabbed Ruth's arm, and we truly were afraid. He marched right up to us and said, "Ladies, you really shouldn't be out on the streets in the dark," and he walked away.

"So much for stereotypes," Ruth and I said to each other. Relief warmed my heart to think our stereotype of him, like most stereotypes, was clearly unjust.

I told Ruth it reminded me of an incident when I was about eight years old. I still lived in Chicago then. My cousin and I were at her piano lesson in a storefront on the north side. She had gone into the studio to practice and left me alone in the front waiting room. An old bum with dirty, uncombed gray hair and ragged clothes, carrying a large box-like tray with a strap supporting it around his neck, walked in the front door. He said something but I didn't hear what.

I said, "Excuse me, sir?"

He walked closer to me and said, "What did you say?"

I wasn't sure what was happening. Was he angry with me? I answered tentatively, "I said, 'Excuse me, sir.'"

He looked me right in the eye and said in a sad kind of voice, "No one's called me 'sir' in years." He handed me a pencil from his tray, turned around, and walked out. A good feeling and a good lesson for an eight-year-old.

I shared this story with Ruth, and then we immediately followed the stranger's advice and found a cab for a quick tour of the capital area until we hooked up with our VW companions as planned and headed home.

Back home, we shared our frustration about Congressman Brown with everyone who would listen. No one was surprised.

* * * * *

Springfield People for Peace worked feverishly to do its part to educate and convince others the war had to be ended. We continued making our presentations, showing our films, organizing vigils, writing letters to the editor, publishing our newsletter, and doing everything we could manage to keep the focus on ending the war. Money was even raised to buy billboard space with a peace sign on it and the message "Peace Is a Victory Too."

We knew what we were doing was probably futile and in the big picture maybe meaningless, but we all felt compelled to do something, to be counted, to stand up for our beliefs. We talked of World War II Germany and its citizens who did nothing during the Holocaust. We shared the story of the boy who threw the starfish back into the ocean, one by one. He couldn't save them all, but he did what he could so some might live.

We spoke of Martin Luther King, Jr., Ghandi, and Jesus and what they taught. We prayed the Prayer of St. Francis of Assisi, "Make Me an Instrument of Thy Peace." Margaret Mead's words inspired me and kept me focused, "Never doubt that a small group of thoughtfully committed citizens can change the world. Indeed, it's the only thing that ever has." We were totally committed in our hearts and minds and found it difficult to understand those who didn't share our concern. We found it even more difficult to understand their anger and hostility.

We wanted people to understand who we were. Treesa Liming, our former chairperson, may have shed some light on this in an interview with the *Springfield News-Sun* published in November 1970:

> *This group represents a real cross section of people. We have parents of boys who have chosen to enlist in the military service, boys who were drafted, boys who have chosen a C.O. (conscientious objector) status, and boys who have gone to Canada rather than serve.*
>
> *We also have couples with no children, parents with children too old and too young to serve.*
>
> *These parents support their sons' decisions, whatever they are, but they also believe that if there is to be peace in the world it is up to the people themselves to make it happen.*

Indeed, we were trying to make it happen.

Chapter Eight

Opportunity Knocks

1971—Nixon continues to withdraw troops but resumes and intensifies the bombing campaign. Agent Orange defoliant used since 1962 discontinued.

Late February 1971, the Paris Peace Talks were stalemated. There had been no formal meetings since U.S. Ambassador David Bruce took over the American delegation in August of 1970.

Three national peace organizations—the American Friends Service Committee (AFSC), the Fellowship of Reconciliation, and Clergy and Laymen Concerned—collaborated to sponsor The Citizens Conference on Ending the War in Indochina to learn first hand what the obstacles were to bringing the war to an end. American citizens from all over the United States would travel to Paris in early March of 1971 to interview the participants at the Paris Peace Talks. The AFSC through Sig Goodman invited Ruth and me to be part of the group.

Go to the Paris Peace Talks? Me? At first, I told Sig there would be no way I could do it—Jim, the kids, the money, my job—but he smiled and asked me to give it some thought. When I told Jim, I expected him to laugh, but he shocked me and didn't hesitate in encouraging me to go. "What an opportunity for you!" he kept repeating. My husband, who'd be left home with our five children (now ages 2 to 8), practically pushed me out the door. *Was he trying to get rid of me?* I vacillated between fear and excitement. Could I really do it? Ruth wasn't so lucky. Her husband opposed her going because of the risks he believed were present in such an undertaking. She didn't buck him. Because Ruth wasn't going, I asked Sig if Karen (my friend who joined Ruth and me at our second meeting) could go in her place. I wasn't sure if I'd have the nerve to go alone. AFSC gave permission, and Karen jumped at the chance. Her husband, Ron, like Jim thought it was a great opportunity. Jim was on his own with our five kids, but Karen's mother, though not happy about Karen's going, took care of their two young sons.

My mother was apprehensive. We'd barely spoken about the war during these years, only seeing each other a couple times a year. When we talked on the phone every Sunday, it was always small talk about family and grandkids. My dad didn't like the phone and hardly ever got on to even say hello, but Mom told me Dad thought my going to the Paris Peace Talks would be a great experience.

Over the years I did learn that they, too, opposed the war, just not actively. Outside of the trip to Paris, they never asked about my peace activities and I didn't tell them. I never knew Jim's parents' feelings about the war, but the absence of any discussion about it led me to believe they still supported the government. The war, or our peace activities, evolved into a forbidden topic with them as it did with most of our relatives. No one wanted to get into a fight over it, including me.

All members of the group paid their own expenses, which were kept to a minimum (about $400). A chartered plane and discounted hotel rate kept the cost within reach although it stretched our budget to the max.

* * * * *

Smilin' Bob's WBLY–AM radio talk show played in homes across Clark County every weekday morning. People could call in and talk about anything from potholes to politics, recipes to religion. Sometimes he'd call people himself to get to the bottom of whatever the problem was. It was the kind of show a lot of people didn't want to admit they listened to, but it reflected the pulse of the community, and people tuned in.

Early one morning, I got a call from Smilin' Bob during his talk show. I hadn't expected him to call me; I was planning to call him later, in a day or two. He had read the press release about our upcoming trip to the Paris Peace Talks in the morning paper.

Smilin' Bob baited me, "You sound like a nice young woman. Now why on earth would you leave your husband and children—was that five of them!—to go traipsing to Paris? For what? Talk to the Vietcong? Consort with the enemy?"

I jockeyed the phone receiver against my shoulder, poured milk into cereal bowls, dished out *the look* commanding silence to the boys, and handed two-year-old Colleen a pretzel to keep her quiet. Eight in the morning was not a good time for me for any radio show interview, let alone one in which I had to defend myself.

"Smilin' Bob," I said as sweetly as I could muster, "my husband *wants* me to go. He's proud that I was invited, and he thinks it'll be a great experience for me. We'll be meeting with *all* the parties at the Paris Peace Talks."

"The Vietcong?" he pressed.

"We're expecting to hear *all* sides as to why this war's still dragging on. We want to know what it'll take to end the war." I swore to myself I'd never be on his show again while home alone with the kids. Four-year-old Patrick dumped his entire cereal bowl into his lap, Colleen wrapped herself around my legs and whined for a drink and attention, and the older boys were late for school.

It had already started as a bad morning. I would have enjoyed telling Smilin' Bob's radio audience what happened earlier. Jim, in his attempt at expediency because he was running so late, asked six-year-old Kevin to bring him his necktie off the doorknob in the family room. After about five minutes, he yelled for Kevin. "What's taking so long?"

A minute later, Kevin ran into the bedroom and handed his dad—the doorknob! He had lifted the tie off the knob and worked the loose screw out of the fitting so he could bring the doorknob to his dad who was running late for work! He heard the word, doorknob, and took it from there. Smilin' Bob could do the same thing with his listeners.

Smilin' Bob asked me to be sure to call in as soon as we returned from the trip. I assured him I would and promised myself it'd be from a quiet room with no distractions—and I wouldn't be in my pajamas!

Every morning after that memorable interview, a firestorm of controversy raged over the air, not over the war, but over two women leaving their families for ten days. All that precious radio time focused on the role of mothers rather than on the war. Most callers thought we were very selfish. This didn't bother us, but we were apprehensive about what we were getting ourselves into. Karen and I kept reassuring each other that if the sponsoring organizations couldn't really set up all the meetings with the various parties at the Peace Talks, we'd still have a trip to Paris. What harm could come to us?

Chapter Nine

The Paris Peace Talks

1971—Nixon encourages a tactical South Vietnamese invasion of Laos. Congress lowers the voting age to 18.

To enhance credibility, the three sponsoring peace organizations that planned our fact-finding mission worked to have a good cross representation of people. Although a majority were indeed "peace people," there were many who were still on the fence, a few hawks, and several people who had family members missing in action or prisoners of war. Our 171-member delegation drew from forty-one states. We ranged from farmers to physicians, clergy to atheist, students to professionals, housewives to ... well, we had one celebrity. Judy Collins, the folk singer, joined our ranks.

The staff from AFSC in Dayton arranged a car pool for us to get to New York. Lloyd Danzeisen, a tall, thin conscientious objector (CO) from World War II, drove. Until then, I didn't even realize there were COs during World War II.

Married with two children, Lloyd was a member of the Church of the Brethren, a recognized peace church. He had served in a CO camp (a leftover from the old Civilian Conservation Corps) in Oregon for two years, 1944 to 1946. He worked as a smoke jumper (fire fighter) or planted trees and built houses. He joked with us about the first person he met when he arrived. The guy came out of a shower and on seeing Lloyd with his Bible in his hand, said, "Oh, no, not another *Holy Joe!*" That man eventually became a Catholic brother.

* * * * *

March 3, 1971. A briefing at Kennedy Airport introduced the staff accompanying us and the itinerary for the coming week. By the time we were to board our flight, I was such a nervous wreck I couldn't leave the restroom. Karen impatiently paced outside the stall door, nagging me, "Come on, Peggy. We're going to miss the plane." That really helped settle me down!

Finally we rushed to the gate where the staff herded us and our fellow delegates toward the plane. One of those barking instructions was a rather large man with a clipboard. Karen and I eyeballed a button on his lapel: "Boycott Fur-Wearing People." Karen, wearing her gray leather coat with a fox collar (her graduation present from her mother), slunk out of his view. "I'm sure glad he isn't coming with us," Karen whispered to me. But his little button caused us big doubts. Did we belong here? Who were all these other people? What was going to happen to us?

We flew Icelandic Air. Shortly after takeoff, I began to feel queasy. Luckily Karen had some air sickness medication with her. Normally it might have made me sleepy but with my adrenaline pumping so hard, I was still wired. People were very friendly and moved about the plane, meeting and greeting one another. Outside of one eighteen-year-old, we appeared to be the youngest members. Karen just turned twenty-five, and I was pushing thirty. (I never did like the counter-culture slogan, "Don't Trust Anybody over 30.") The majority were middle-aged plus. We took our cue from them and began to meet and greet the others. These other delegates exuded a quiet confidence, and I began to feel less nervous and more excited. Everyone was full of anticipation as to whether or not the very impressive agenda we were given would actually happen.

After a forty-five-minute stopover in Iceland, we landed in Luxembourg the following morning. A harrowing eight-hour bus ride through the narrow hilly roads of northern France convinced us that French drivers earned the title of craziest drivers in the world, at least French bus drivers. The rolling hills of the French countryside were beautiful, but the roads were narrow and the bus so fast, we were all terrified. Tree branches constantly hit against the side of the bus. Once we passed so close to a bicyclist, her long hair brushed our windows. Everyone breathed a sigh of relief when the girl wasn't run over. Our silent individual fears rose in a collective audible prayer of thanks.

Our hotel, the Hotel Garnier, was modest but pleasant. Our room, lackluster in beige and brown, mirrored our exhausted selves. The postered twin beds sat so high, I thought I'd need a step stool. The tiled bathroom had a bidet. Karen explained its use to me. Karen being more experienced, or at least having more experienced parents, knew to bring her own toilet paper. It was a very good idea. The stuff in the room was like waxy brown paper.

The agenda indicated we'd be meeting with all parties involved in the Paris Peace Talks:

- Republic of Vietnam (South Vietnam)
- Democratic Republic of Vietnam (North Vietnam)
- Provisional Revolutionary Government of the Republic of South Vietnam (PRG), also known as the National Liberation Front (NLF) or Vietcong
- Americans
- Buddhists, Catholics, international press, Laotians and Cambodians who weren't represented at the talks.

With every minute of every day scheduled so tightly, we knew we'd only view Paris after 11 P.M. No free time other than sleep time.

* * * * *

March 5, 1971. Our first meeting was the next morning, Friday, at the North Vietnamese Embassy. An unassuming three-story brick house with a black wrought-iron fence, it was crowded in between two identical houses and didn't meet my expectation of an embassy. Photographers and newspeople gathered on the sidewalk as our group filed inside. After climbing several flights of stairs, we crowded into a large reception room with a couple of fireplaces and rows of folding chairs. It was a tight squeeze for 171 Americans. Vietnamese men in suits and women in long brightly colored dresses greeted us. Most of them spoke English. We felt welcomed to their home rather than their embassy.

Minister Xuan Thuy, leader of the Democratic Republic of Vietnam (North Vietnam) delegation, invited us to take pictures and use our tape recorders. He was often on the evening news, and I was certainly full of awe for participating in a piece of history. Not that we were making history, but we were meeting people who were.

Minister Xuan Thuy welcomed us with "a warm greeting to those who have come so far," but blasted the resumption of the bombing of Hanoi. He spent a lot of time reviewing the history of the war. I listened carefully for distortions but found it was the same history I had studied.

"Nixon," he said, "insists on mutual withdrawal as he claims North Vietnam has made aggression. Can troops of Washington make aggression in New York? Planes fly to see what's going on in North Vietnam. Can North Vietnam fly over the United States?" He insisted on a date being set for complete withdrawal of U.S. troops. "If the United States doesn't have enough carriers to bring troops all home," he added, "I'm sure they can borrow them."

While he spoke, I scratched my arms, my legs, my neck. "My God, you're covered with hives," Karen diagnosed. I never had them before in my whole life, and I really wasn't feeling that nervous now. I was even able to stay out of the bathroom! Again lucky for me, Karen had some Benadryl (prescription only back then) with her. Her father, a doctor, had given her some, just in case. It did its magic. The hives disappeared.

We discovered why we were scheduled there for the whole day. With 171 visitors and only one bathroom, it'd take all day to shuffle us through. The bathroom was as small as mine at home, and hanging on a clothesline stretched across the tub were several pairs of men's black socks. *Were they trying to win us over with this touch of hominess?*

Lunch was Vietnamese food that looked too foreign to me to even try. A logistical nightmare in the small quarters, Karen and I decided to skip lunch and didn't even take a plate. Many of our group enjoyed the lunch though. (Later that week, I'd have paid $10 for just one Big Mac.)

After Minister Xuan Thuy spoke, his subordinates filled the rest of the day. Vietnamization (Nixon's policy of gradually withdrawing U.S. troops and turning the fighting over to the South Vietnamese), they said, meant prolongation and extension of the war. They also criticized the U.S. pacification program (intended to secure the countryside), which bulldozed villages in South Vietnam and concentrated people in strategic hamlets surrounded by barbed wire, as brutal.

The North Vietnamese position called for a ten-point solution, primarily the withdrawal of all foreign troops and abandonment of the U.S.–supported South Vietnamese leaders, President (General) Nguyen Van Thieu and Vice President Nguyen Cao Ky (formerly South Vietnam air force commander and prime minister). "We ask for the right of self-determination," one leader said. "War is not in the south of the United States."

Time was allowed for questions and answers. Overall we found our hosts to be hospitable and caring about what we thought of them. They did not treat us like their enemy, but we knew it was in their self-interest to gain our sympathies. The bottom line for the day was for the United States to set a date and withdraw from Vietnam. Our members asking questions on behalf of prisoners of war were assured all POWs would be returned as soon as

U.S. troops pulled out. Of course, we had no basis for believing this.

That evening we watched some propaganda films describing the Vietnamese people and their search for peace. Everyone in our delegation seemed to be marking time in assessing what they believed and didn't believe. We still had four more days of listening and asking. We were free at 11 P.M. to do a little sightseeing or go to bed. Karen and I decided we'd catch up on our sleep back in the States. We were going to see as much of Paris as we could.

* * * * *

March 6, 1971. Saturday we returned to the same building to hear Madame Nguyen Thi Binh, Minister of Foreign Affairs and head of the delegation to the Paris Peace Talks for the Provisional Revolutionary Government (sometimes called the National Liberation Front or Vietcong). She also appeared on the evening news often, and I marveled that a woman held such a high political seat. She was an attractive woman who spoke softly. An interpreter translated for her. "Your bombs have destroyed the cradles of our children and the graves of our ancestors," she said to a room of absolute quiet. "One-half ton of high explosive bombs have fallen on us for each man, woman, and child. . . . " She smiled when she told about some GIs who saw written on a wall in some village, "Americans Go Home." Underneath the soldiers added, "As soon as possible." Her lighthearted remark helped salve my raw emotions and battered conscience.

That evening we went to the University of Paris to hear the Laotians. Again, it was sightseeing after 11 P.M. It was so late, so dark, and we so tired, that I have only fleeting memories of the River Seine, the Arch de Triumph, and Pagalle, a famous spot for hookers where one commented she knew we were Americans because of our shoes.

* * * * *

March 7, 1971. Sunday we returned to the university where we heard two touching and credible speakers although they weren't participants at the peace talks. A Buddhist monk, Venerable Thich Nhat Hanh of the Unified Buddhist Church spoke and moved me to tears as he described the war and the suffering. A deeply spiritual man, he pointed out that communism and anticommunism represented only a small educated segment of the Vietnamese people, 80 percent of whom were Buddhists. He added, "The spirit of man is mutilated both in the socialist camp and in that of the capitalists." Taking a strong stand against the policies and propaganda of the Nixon administration, he begged for a cease fire. "Vietnamization means changing the color of the corpses," he said.

"The United States holds the power and capacity to end this war," he continued. "If American people try hard they will be able to end the war. This does not require the defeat of the United States or honor of the United States. Only concessions. We want a cease fire that does not need to be negotiated. They just stop. An end to the killing will bring about an atmosphere for political settlement. I am trying to speak for the majority of peasants not represented in Paris. The United States might have to set a date for total withdrawal but to ignore the desire for immediate cease fire is to ignore the suffering of man. So do what you can to create the pressure on your government to end the war. Demand your government set the date to withdraw." None of us knew then that the war would drag on for four more bloody years.

The second speaker was Father Nguyen Dinh Thi, a Vietnamese Catholic priest. "Less than 10 percent of the Vietnamese population is Catholic," he began. "There are eleven bishops and a seminary in North Vietnam, but the Vatican has cut off all relations with them. This was a political move rather than a religious one. Religious freedom is respected in North Vietnam. . . . The Archbishop of Saigon (in the South) declared that South Vietnamese Catholics do not want an anticommunism crusade. They want peace. . . . Many Catholics were on the side of the

French and fled south because of their fears of communism. Now some still fear but many believe they can coexist and they do."

He talked of the country being one and how Catholics from North Vietnam fled to the south when American planes dropped flyers saying the "Virgin Mary Fled South." He described families who were split between the north and south, fighting on opposite sides only because of where they lived, not because of what they believed. He said he and other church leaders used to see communism as the devil's work; they now believed they all could coexist. A coalition government for the whole of Vietnam was the solution.

As soon as Fr. Nguyen finished speaking and left the stage, I hurried to meet him. My Catholicism outweighed my timidity. A priest, Fr. James Murphy, from New York happened to do the same, and we met Fr. Nguyen together. After chatting briefly, Fr. Nguyen invited the American priest and me to join him for lunch at his house. Without hesitation, I said I'd love to. I raced back to Karen and told her what I was doing. I'd miss part of the meeting with the representatives of the international press, but she could cover that for me. I didn't give her a chance to argue with me.

The two priests and I walked eight blocks to an old, shabby house. The three of us discreetly ignored a man urinating on the sidewalk as we passed. The Catholic Vietnamese group occupied a small, sparsely furnished apartment on an upper floor. Fr. Nguyen introduced us to several other priests. We sat in a small parlor and talked about the war and their feelings about the communists. Fr. Nguyen said, "At one time, we saw the communists as devils and feared them very much. But now we see them only as men, and we can deal with men. We couldn't deal with the devil." I nodded in agreement. I understood.

Fr. Nguyen invited us into the dining room. Several women rushed about carrying fish, rice, and vegetables. We sat at a huge oblong table that took up the entire room. I'd guess about twenty Vietnamese priests (most of whom only spoke French and Vietnamese) sat around the table, all eyes on the two Americans.

They made room for us and as I sat down, Fr. Nguyen asked if I'd like some wine. I politely said, "No thank you."

He then asked if I wanted some coffee.

"No thank you," I answered again.

"Would you like some tea?"

"No thank you," I said shaking my head and feeling more and more like the Ugly American. I couldn't bring myself to say yes when I knew I'd never be able to even fake drinking wine, coffee, or tea.

"Beer?" Everyone's eyes were on me. Beer was even worse, and I bowed my head a bit and said once again, "No thank you."

Exasperated, he asked, "What *do* you drink?"

I looked up and answered, "Coca-Cola."

With that, in unison, all twenty-some Vietnamese priests shook their index fingers toward each other, nodded their heads knowingly, and murmured, "Ahh, Coca-Cola!" It would have been a great commercial. We all laughed and I remained drinkless.

During lunch, a young, good-looking, and boyish, Vietnamese man with big horn-rimmed glasses joined us. A former seminarian, he was on his way to the Vatican in Rome, hoping to escape serving in the South Vietnamese Army if he could keep his visa. He had a brother-in-law in the North Vietnamese Army and one in the South Vietnamese Army. He spoke excellent English and offered to show us the way back to the university. His name was Tam.

Tam had the slight and beautiful features of the Vietnamese people, his dark eyes radiating friendship and interest. We shared stories of our families and the church. Originally from the north, Tam's father had served in the French army and had been killed. Tam was eight years old when his mother moved the family to the south as part of the huge exodus of Catholics in 1954. His married sister remained in the north and freely practiced her Catholic religion. His mother, Tam explained, as were many Catholics, was very influenced by the French and chose to live in a Catholic village in the south where they enjoyed an economic advantage over the non-Catholics.

Somehow I wanted to keep talking with him and hear about him and his family. I felt so connected to him. Like the young black men who hitched their way in my car, he represented more to me than just another person. Again, I wanted him to know how much I cared about his people—all people. I wanted Karen to meet him so I asked if he'd like to join us that evening to help show us around. Sunday evening we'd be free at 9 P.M. instead of the usual 11. He didn't hesitate and promised he'd meet us at our hotel.

Fr. Murphy and I returned to the university in time to hear Minister Chau Seng of the United Front of Cambodia pepper his history of Cambodia with comments like, "If you want to fight communism, why not go to Moscow?" After his lengthy talk about Chinese and American relations, he summed up by saying America has a great history and a great people. "If you take your troops out of Vietnam, we will roll out the red carpet for you," he boasted. An American businessman jumped up in the audience, waved his hand, and called out, "Can we sell you the red carpet?" It felt so good to laugh again!

That evening, Tam, Karen, and I walked along the Seine and absorbed some of the flavor of Paris. We returned to the hotel and joined a small group including Judy Collins. We sat in a small anteroom telling our stories and listening to Tam. It seemed to me we all wanted to hold on to him a bit longer. Finally, Judy asked us if we'd like to sing. We formed a circle, arms crossed in front of us holding hands Girl Scout style, and swaying to the music. Tam sang some Vietnamese peace songs and translated the words for us. More than a few tears flowed. If it wasn't emotional enough for us already, Judy led us in a final song, "Amazing Grace." It was a true spiritual experience for me.

In our hotel room that night, I was particularly homesick. I had never been away from the family before and being unable to call home made it more difficult. I assumed the cost would be prohibitive and also was afraid of the language barrier. I didn't even try to call, nor did Karen. I remember holding pictures of the kids and aching inside. *How were they doing? Were they all okay? Wait until Jim hears all I have to tell him.* I was so glad Karen was with me.

Several times throughout the week our group met at the Modern Palace Hotel, for "plenary" or open sessions to discuss all we had heard and seen. The organizers followed a Quaker tradition ensuring that our group operated by consensus, a time-consuming process, but one that allowed for all voices to be heard and respected. We had listened hard to the talks, taken notes, and now discussed what we heard. But meeting Vietnamese people face to face and talking with them about the suffering in Vietnam, made what seemed an intellectual or moral or political problem, a reality that ached deep inside us.

* * * * *

March 8, 1971. The South Vietnamese embassy, a majestic building reeking of money with crystal chandeliers, pillars, marble floors, and gold-framed paintings, contrasted sharply with the simple North Vietnamese embassy we visited earlier in the week. Were our tax dollars paying for all this grandeur? We met in a large ballroom with one long wall lined with French doors—and CIA agents? We whispered among ourselves about the well-built, handsome young American men dressed in dark suits, standing ramrod straight, with even straighter faces, placed strategically near the doors. We didn't think their little ear pieces meant they were deaf.

While waiting for Ambassador Pham Dang Lam, head of the Republic of Vietnam (Saigon/South Vietnam) delegation to speak, we were shown two films, one which really insulted our intelligence. It simply paraded all the military hardware boasted by Saigon (funded by the United States) much like a miser might show off his gold. I said to Karen, "It's like a movie created for high school boys itching to go off to war." Later a Vietnam veteran told us it was the same film shown in boot camp.

As a group, we became more and more agitated by the tasteless propaganda pressed upon us. Frustration mounted as Ambassador Pham parroted the same simplistic line we had heard over and over at home, fight for freedom and democracy and stop communism.

He focused on the atrocities of the north and Vietcong. A black woman finally stood up saying, "You keep talkin' about North Vietnamese. Honey, I'm talkin' about North Americans!" He ignored her statement and continued speaking in his excellent English, telling us the countryside is pacified, elections are honest, and Cambodia and Laos have been great military victories.

A farmer from Illinois summed it up for all our delegation when he addressed Ambassador Pham, "We came because of humanitarian reasons, because we love you. We even love these CIA agents and that ain't easy!" Everyone laughed and clapped. Some gave the peace sign to the red-faced agents. Yes, they actually blushed!

The farmer then continued, "Your brothers, and our brothers, at the other embassy have shown us films of anticommunist troops shooting prisoners with their hands tied behind their backs. You have shown us films of mass graves at Hue[2], and I suspect both may have happened. This is why we are against this war, because it turns men into beasts, and in the name of God, it must be stopped! Please prepare yourselves to seek peaceful solutions without continued American military intervention because we are going home!" We applauded his remarks.

Totally frustrated and angry at the futility of the session, though many still managed to smile at or acknowledge the CIA agents still posted at the doors, we dragged ourselves out of the building into the fresh sunlight. On our own for lunch, Karen and I ate at a sidewalk cafe that

---

[2]Thousands of Vietnamese killed by Vietcong during Easter offensive in village of Hue.

felt more Parisian than anything else so far. Karen, with her two years of high school French and me at her side, stopped at a hat store to buy Ron a *chapeau*. We had been warned the French didn't much like Americans who wouldn't at least try to speak their language. Karen, laughing at her own feeble attempts to speak French, won the sales clerk over while I remained as invisible as I could. I never did shop in Paris (didn't have any money anyway).

That afternoon we visited the American Embassy. Ambassador David Bruce would only speak with twelve members of our group, and Karen and I were not part of the chosen twelve. The general feeling among all delegates was one of disgust and dismay that our own ambassador wouldn't address the entire group. To top it off, our democratic government's representatives banned cameras and tape recorders, something permitted in all previous meetings. How un-American!

Two assistants to Ambassador Bruce addressed our entire delegation. The room where we met looked like an IBM computer room, very sterile, sleek, black and white. They stood behind a long wooden table, and we were seated classroom style.

One of them during his long address floored us with the statement, "Communism is not monolithic." Karen and I looked at each other in disbelief. *If it wasn't monolithic, meaning communism was not under the united control of any one country or belief system, then why the war?* Our government had always preached communism was one evil force taking over the world, and Russia was the real enemy. It was all part of what our government called the Domino Theory: A communist victory in Vietnam would lead to the fall of the neighboring countries to communism. That was why Vietnam was important to us. We had to stop the spread of communism before it spread to us. Now our own representative at the Paris Peace Talks admitted this was not the problem.

The question-and-answer period was very intense with the ambassador's assistants unable to refute facts as we presented them. This affirmed for me that the information that led me to change my position from hawk to dove was indeed the truth. When he flat out denied the threat of the Domino Theory, I was dumbfounded. *Then why were we in Vietnam at all? It was the only reason that had made any sense—fighting communism in our own self-interest.* Our question of how to end the war went unanswered. There was no concrete response to our questions regarding the north's position of the United States setting a date for withdrawal of all American troops and discontinuing support for the South Vietnamese leaders, President Nguyen Van Thieu and Vice President Nguyen Cao Ky. As I see it now, that's what eventually happened. It took two more years of bloodshed before Nixon set the date and brought all our troops home (March 1973). The war officially ended another bloody year and half after that with the collapse of Saigon on April 30, 1975.

As our stressful session with the Americans came to an end, Judy Collins began singing, "All we are saying, is give peace a chance." Everyone stood and joined in countless and tearful repetitions of the same verse. "All we are saying, is give peace a chance." Karen and I stood right behind the court stenographers (three men in suits) who also stood but kept clicking away on their keys, recording every single verse we sang.

* * * * *

March 9, 1971. Tuesday, our last day in Paris, we attended a question-and-answer session with the North Vietnamese and the Provisional Revolutionary Government/National Liberation Front. They remained steadfast in their earlier position of setting a date for withdrawal. Now thirty years later, my most vivid memory of that session is of a nun sitting in the first row, sound asleep while the speaker answered questions. It was a very un-nunly thing to do.

That afternoon there was a plenary session followed by discussion groups. The focus of the dialogue deteriorated into a heated exchange about possible repercussions the delegates might face at home if they signed a telegram to President Nixon detailing what we believed necessary to stop the war. Some were afraid to sign it.

Two German-American women spoke up, chastising those who expressed their personal fears. The first woman apologized for her foreign accent and then said:

> *I'm grew up under Nazi Germany. I know what it is to live in a totalitarian government . . . and I'm deeply discouraged to hear time and again from you that you are afraid of what will happen to you at home. You remember that after the Second World War there was the Nuremberg Trial, and the German people, not just those who made the war—all of them—were accused of having been in accord of putting the Jews into the gas chambers, and having committed all those war crimes along with those who actually did it. We know that we are committing crimes in this war. All of us, even the people here, sitting here will be held guilty for it. So I think we should once forget what could happen to our jobs, what can happen to our lives, what can happen to our children. If we that believe so much in peace don't put our lives now on the line for this, and don't all of us sign this telegram to the President—at least—then I think we haven't accomplished anything.*

When she finished another German woman spoke:

> *I have lost my family in a Germany concentration camp, and I have been reared in Germany. I lived through all the war and heard people say, "We didn't know; we didn't know." But we know and have the responsibility to stand up. . . .*

With just a few dissenting, the group adopted the following statement that was sent by telegram to President Nixon on March 11, 1971.

> *We, who have come together from throughout the United States and are now returning from a week of dis-*

cussions in Paris with the representatives of each of the four delegations to the Paris Talks and other interested Indochinese parties, urge you, Mr. President, to stop the war by:
1) setting a date for the immediate and total withdrawal of all U.S. military personnel from Indochina. This will assure an immediate cease fire for U.S. forces in Indochina and the negotiations for the release of American prisoners of war: and
2) by discontinuing military, economic, and political support for Thieu, Ky, and Khiem whose government is unrepresentative of the people of South Vietnam. This will pave the way to a cease fire between the Vietnamese and to a political settlement among the Indochinese peoples. We have become convinced in Paris that present American military policy can lead only to a prolongation of this bloody war and to untold suffering for the Indochinese and American peoples; and, further invites the reaction of other countries in the area, including the Peoples Republic of China.

Karen and I both signed the statement. Six of the 171 delegates did not.

Fr. Nguyen, the priest who spoke on Sunday, invited all Catholic members of our delegation to dinner (at the house where I had lunch with him) on our last evening in Paris. Three nuns, Fr. Murphy, and a handful of other lay people attended.

I had volunteered to do some typing for our conference sponsors earlier that afternoon. They sent me by cab to another part of Paris where I spent about an hour typing some materials for our use on the trip home. Someone wrote down Fr. Nguyen's address so I could take a cab directly there when finished. It sounded simple enough, but after I left the apartment, I found myself caught in rush hour traffic. Never having even hailed a cab in the United States, I lost all confidence at the sight of the traffic. What was worse, I wanted to ask for help, but I couldn't speak one word of French. Already late for the dinner, I clutched my scrap of paper with the address on it and wandered aimlessly trying to spy an empty cab. If I had any heady feelings about being part of this historical adventure, I now felt like sitting on the curb and crying like a lost kindergartner. I didn't even know how to catch a cab. After the initial rush hour traffic thinned, I finally stepped into the street and waved at every cab that passed. Eventually one stopped. I handed him my note—or was it pinned to my shirt?—and simply nodded when he repeated the address. It was an act of faith.

When I walked into the dining room, six two-liter bottles of Coca-Cola stood in a line on the long table. I laughed with delight and tried to explain the significance to the others. Dinner was American style; chicken and gravy, potatoes, fish, salad, lunch meat, and French bread. Many of the Vietnamese who joined us that evening could speak a little English and Fr. Murphy bridged the gap with his French. We lingered at the table, laughing at times but always conscious of the war and its toll on the Vietnamese people as well as our own. By the end of the evening, we created our own peace treaty. That's all we wanted. Peace.

Later that night, Tam, a couple others from the dinner, and I joined Karen at the hotel and stopped in all-night cafes and bars that Tam was familiar with. We couldn't bring ourselves to go to bed and simply leave in the morning. At sunrise, we returned to the hotel, and Tam waited with us until the bus took us on the long trip to the Luxembourg airport. Tam and I corresponded a bit after I got back home, but then we lost contact. I never knew what became of him.

Karen and I slept the entire bus ride and most of the flight home. I imagine a lot of others did too but I was too asleep to notice.

* * * * *

It was a fun and emotional homecoming with Jim and the kids, but I desperately needed rest. The first night home in my own bed, I must have had a bit of jet lag and some kind of bug. I woke up in the middle of the night, barely making it to the bathroom before I "lost my cookies." As I headed back to the bedroom, I, who never got sick, fainted. I fell dead away and as I came to—I wasn't hurt—I heard Jim's footsteps. Jim, a sound sleeper who never once heard a baby cry, actually heard me fall! He'd be shocked to see me lying on the floor; he'd be so worried, so concerned. I envisioned him agonizing, leaning over me, "Peg, Peg, what's wrong?" I decided to stay put and let him fuss over me. Next thing I knew, though, I was looking up at Jim as he stepped over me; he stepped right over me without missing a beat! He didn't say a word; he just kept walking. I pulled myself up when I realized he wasn't coming back to my rescue. *Why didn't he help me? Why didn't he fuss over me? What was wrong with him?* I found him lying on the floor of the bathroom. Halfway between consciousness and sleepwalking, I guessed he was fine. Surprisingly, I was too.

The next day Karen and I immediately began writing the speech we'd share with as many Springfielders as we could find to listen.

Chapter Ten

Sharing the Experience

> *1971—In the fall, President Nixon orders U.S. soldiers to be assigned only to defensive roles. U.S. military personnel in South Vietnam at the end of the year: 156,800.*

Our experience in Paris made the front-page headline of the Springfield paper: *Firm Vietnam Withdrawal Date 'Must,' Mothers Feel.* Karen and I gathered at her house (in a quiet room with no kids) and called Smilin' Bob. The first words out of his mouth were, "I'm the first one to ask you what you think of about Lt. Calley and the court martial." The My Lai massacre of 300 unarmed men, women, children, and elderly had happened two years earlier. Lt. Calley's trial was just ending. We wanted to talk about ending the war, not that tragedy. "We want to talk to you about what we learned in Paris," I said firmly, and we did.

After our radio interview, we began booking speaking engagements with local service clubs, churches, and schools. Due to the publicity we received, we eventually were able to set up over thirty different talks, morning, noon, and evening. We saw this as the most important part of our entire mission, although it was one we both dreaded. Public speaking, often ranked second only to a root canal, is bad enough even when the topic isn't controversial. I'd have preferred the root canal.

Our first speaking engagement was at Karen's adult Sunday school class. It didn't go well. One member of the class whose brother had served in Vietnam became incensed. "You Communists!" she screamed at us as she slammed out of the classroom. The young minister shook his head in way of an apology and in an effort to restore some peace to the classroom played a tape, "Amazing Grace" by Judy Collins. Of all the songs he could have chosen; tears poured down our cheeks. We had so many more speaking engagements arranged. Were we strong enough?

In each of our presentations, we stuck to our fifteen-minute prepared speech and took questions afterwards. We were always met with mixed reactions, from distanced disinterest (people not even looking at us while we spoke) to outright hostility to genuine concern. More than once we were told it was who we were—middle-class housewives, high heels and all, not long-haired hippies—that they were able to hear us. Able to listen. We told ourselves we were making a difference.

Sometimes we couldn't dodge the label Communist. Once after Sunday Mass, a local city commissioner came up to me in front of my children. She waved her finger in my face and disgustedly spat out the word at me, "Communist!" I ignored her and reassured my kids it was no big deal. She was just angry.

Without a doubt, the worst time Karen and I had was at one of our county's rural schools, Northwestern High School. We had been invited to speak to a general assembly first thing in the morning and then would go to various history classes throughout the day.

Surprisingly it was standing room only in the auditorium. We gave our speech and then opened it for questions and answers. A man identified himself as a history teacher and made a comment about "might making right." It didn't matter what our country did as long as it could do it. I responded with some remarks about morality and Hitler. He angrily called me a "Pollyanna." The entire auditorium burst into applause in support of him. It took all my willpower to keep from breaking into tears. This should have been a tip-off for what kind of day it was going to be.

As we went from class to class (we didn't even have a free period for lunch), a group of four to six boys followed us into each classroom, for no other reason but to harass us, interrupting and making rude moans and groans as we spoke. These kids were trying to intimidate us. Why they were allowed to skip their other classes is beyond me. Why the teachers didn't put them out is beyond me. Why we didn't have enough sense to protest their presence is beyond me, but we didn't. We put up with their rude behavior all day.

Finally it was the last period of the day. Karen and I dragged into the classroom and found ourselves surrounded by Nazi swastikas, flags, and posters all embracing Nazi Germany, and, small surprise, the same man who preached "might makes right" that morning was the teacher. (Later I learned he liked to submerge his class in the feel of the period they were studying.) He sat in the back of the class and did not make any comments. The boys who followed us all day were from his class, the last period of the day. The boys refrained from their obnoxious behavior and just glared at us. Maybe they were as worn out as we were. When the final bell rang, we escaped to our car and said a prayer of thanks that it was over, and that we didn't live in that school district.

This encounter didn't help the anxiety I suffered every time we had a presentation. I'd be so nervous I couldn't eat all day; it made a great weight-control program. Many times, prior to our speaking, Karen paced outside the restroom door begging me to hurry up.

A tangible tension hung in the room during each engagement, but overall, people were polite with heartfelt question-and-answer periods as they wrestled with their own feelings about the war. One time, after our talk, a woman raced after us, screaming "Communists," as she followed us into the parking lot. My first instinct was to see if she had a weapon. She didn't, and we hurried into our car with no further problem.

Later we learned we were probably the most active speakers from the entire delegation. Sig, who recommended us as part of the delegation, took great pride in his protégés. And for us, we took pride in our experience and pride in Springfield People for Peace, pushing our message for peace. However, we knew it wasn't enough, that it would never be enough.

Chapter Eleven

Banned

1971—Vietnam Veterans Against the War hold a large demonstration in Washington, D.C. that is part of one of the largest mass demonstrations in U.S. history.

Enthusiasm ran high within our group. Memorial Day 1971: Not only were we going to be in the Memorial Day parade, but we'd throw a "peace festival" in Snyder Park with bands and speakers. We planned a float with the theme, "Let Freedom Ring—For All People" and decided to pull our kids alongside in wagons. We had been in previous Memorial Day parades but had never considered a float. This would be special. It would be fun to work together on something so positive.

But then came the bombshell. Just a week before the parade, we were banned from participating. The reason? We had decided to wear black arm bands, and an article in the newspaper publicizing our participation had mentioned it. We were stunned. We never dreamed it would cause a problem. Ruth and I called on Roger Sharp, Clark County Veterans Service Officer, to talk with him about reconsidering. We offered to march without the armbands because that seemed to be the sticking point for the Clark County Veterans Council. We explained we were basically a group of mothers and our kids.

However, we found out the real problem was *us:* war protesters. It didn't matter who we were. Mr. Sharp could barely contain his anger and outrage. He was the parade marshall, and the Memorial Day parade was his baby. Sitting behind his desk, he lambasted us as communist dupes and roared at us about carrying his "razor-sharp sword." If we came to the parade, his men "in hard hats and brass knuckles" would be there. It was a surreal meeting.

Headlines in the next morning's paper proclaimed: "Peace Marchers Out." A member of the Veterans Council said, "It just wouldn't be right. We are honoring the dead. We don't want them marching in the parade with black armbands."

The article quoted Mr. Sharp as saying we had obtained permission from the council to participate, but our recently announced intentions were entirely different from what we had contracted for. He feared that undesirable elements might cause a disruptive confrontation and that led him to revoke permission.

The paper continued: "Mr. Sharp cited friction between the veterans' groups and radical students who might try to join the march as the source of concern. A number of 'hard hats' marched with last year's parade to prevent disruption, but no such precautions are planned for Monday."

Radical students? The controversy swirled over the local radio station. Smilin' Bob polled everyone who called in. The results? Nothing scientific but there certainly was no groundswell of support for us. In the end, however, we generated more publicity than we ever would have had we been in the parade.

Ruth wrote in a letter to the editor in the Springfield paper, *"It is a strange world indeed where antiwar sentiments are unpatriotic and intolerable. Is it not possible to honor the men who died unselfishly and yet to hate the war they died in?"*

In the same letter, she quoted a wounded Vietnam soldier, *"There is no glory in war. When the power of love replaces the love of power, we will have peace."* Powerful words!

Gratefully the superintendent of parks did not withdraw permission for our peace festival held after the parade. The newspaper reported several hundred people attended the event. Six different bands donated their time as did a myriad of speakers including clergy, veterans, students, professors, and Karen and me. People (again a good cross section of the community) picnicked, clapped to the music, cheered the speakers, and felt a kinship united in a cause. Our kids picked up trash. By the end of the day, we congratulated one another on another job well done.

For me, it was a bittersweet time. My husband's father had died that morning, and Jim had left two days earlier to be with him. Once the festival ended and we helped clean up the park area, I packed the five kids in the car and we drove back to Chicago.

I chuckle now to look at a May 30, 1978, newspaper article featuring Mr. Sharp and that year's very successful Memorial Day parade. For some reason, he brought up the parade back in 1971 and took credit for *not canceling* it because of the possibility of violence. He reported he had fifty men in hard hats marching along the curbs. (He didn't mention brass knuckles!) Then he went on to say that several protesters thought better of their plans, and the *demonstration* was called off. Funny the different perspective he had from ours.

Chapter Twelve

Pressing On

1971—Publication of stolen portions of the Pentagon Papers, a defense department analysis of the war through 1967, exposes government lies about the war. United States drops three times the total tonnage of bombs during all of World War II on Vietnam during the thirty months of Nixon's presidency.

That summer of 1971, Ruth received a call from a woman in neighboring Champaign County who asked if she could come to talk with us at our next meeting. I remember the moment Dorothy Franke, and her husband, Arthur, both gray haired and dressed in suits, breezed into Ruth's living room and immediately commanded our attention, respect, and admiration. *Maybe it's just the hat she's wearing,* I thought. No, it was their very presence, their energy, and as we were to learn, their commitment.

Dorothy was to become our collective mentor and role model, a role she's continued for the past thirty years. Unlike most of us, Dorothy had always been a peace person. She said it started in high school long before World War II. Self-described as an introverted girl who'd slink along the halls if anyone looked at her twice, she was shocked to be chosen for the debate team.

In her junior year, she had given a speech about poor and distressed women (they didn't call them abused women then) during the depression. The following year, Dorothy's senior year, the president of her class (1935) nominated her to be on the debate team. He had been impressed with the way she could speak.

With no knowledge of the subject, she found herself assigned to the pro side of "Resolved that the nations should agree to prevent the international shipment of arms and munitions." In her rebuttal, she proclaimed with conviction, "The crosses, row after row in Arlington National Cemetery, are dollar signs to the munitions makers." The other side won. But in later life, she always traced the birth of her peaceful endeavors to that debate when she was seventeen years old.

When ground troops were first sent to Vietnam in 1965, Dorothy began a letter-writing campaign in opposition to the buildup. Later, although she and Arthur farmed in St. Paris (Ohio), they participated in the weekly vigils in downtown Dayton about 30 miles away.

On three separate occasions they marched in Washington, D.C. On their first march in 1969, she saw clouds of tear gas and realized they, as older citizens, were never the target for tear gas, only the young people. One time when they went with a group on chartered buses, other participants parked their car at the Brethren Church on Salem Avenue in Dayton. Arthur was adamant about parking under the street light. When they returned from D.C., they found someone had slit all the tires on all cars except theirs.

Once Dorothy appeared as a guest on the *Phil Donahue Show* in Dayton. With a son in Vietnam, Dorothy spoke as a mother who opposed the war. Another woman, whose son was also in Vietnam, spoke in favor of the government's policy. Dorothy felt sad about this other woman and her unquestioning support of the war. About two months after the show, this same woman phoned Dorothy, introduced herself, and simply said, "Mrs. Franke, I want to tell you, you were right," and hung up before Dorothy could say a word.

Springfield People for Peace continued its push to end the war through films, speakers, vigils, demonstrations, and the press. Our meetings reflected the commitment our members felt. We were never short of volunteers to take responsibility for various activities. In July of 1971, we sponsored a National Priorities Caravan and in September that year the Indochina Mobile Education Project.

The caravan, sponsored by the Dayton Regional Office of the American Friends Service Committee, consisted of four members who traveled to different communities in the Midwest. In each town, they conducted a two-week series of activities on the need for reordering national and local priorities. Springfield People for Peace invited the caravan to Springfield and Mayor Robert Pyle helped welcome the clean cut and energetic young men (one was a former Green Beret) and women with a picnic celebration at Snyder Park. Speaking engagements were scheduled with churches and service clubs on issues including national priorities, the military-industrial complex, and directions for American democracy.

One discussion program, conducted at the Fifth Lutheran Church, focused on the role of the minister in social change. One minister, quoted in the *Springfield News-Sun,* asked, "How do you combat a small town, rural mentality which says that President Nixon is surrounded by the smartest men in the world, and therefore we must follow everything he does?"

I wonder now, after the truth is out about these "smartest" men and their lies, if that mentality still exists? It probably does. Because I even find myself still wanting to believe our government leaders—but then I remember Vietnam. I question everything now.

The minister continued to say, "It scares me because this was the attitude which prevailed in Germany prior to World War II."

The caravaneers knocked on almost a thousand doors asking families to reply to a questionnaire about tax money and priorities. Three Wittenberg faculty members supervised the entire survey process. An open forum was held to present the results of the survey. Of the 250 completed questionnaires (a good, legitimate random sample), housing and urban renewal was listed as the number one most pressing problem facing Springfield. Eighty-six percent of those responding favored U.S. withdrawal from Indochina. Other data covered areas such as natural resources; economic development; and health, education and welfare. For two weeks, these young volunteers inspired and affirmed us.

Our brand-new Upper Valley Mall allowed us to host the "Indochina Exhibit" in the concourse the weekend of September 10, 1971, at no charge! Don Luce, an agricultural economist who lived in Indochina for twelve years, prepared the exhibit to present a side of the war that was not only heartrending but essential for the American people to understand.

The exhibit was an amazing collection of striking artwork, photographs, slides, and films reflecting the cultures and life in Indochina. The display commanded attention from shoppers passing by. It included pictures of the bamboo "tiger cages" Luce discovered being used for POWs on one of South Vietnam's largest island prisons. Right after his discovery, his visa was revoked by the Saigon government, and he was forced to leave.

About this same time, one of our active members, Jean Martensen, a tall, blue-eyed blonde mother of two young daughters, coordinated a "No-buy effort" locally as part of a nationwide effort to urge the federal government to end the Vietnam War. Women were asked to do all their shopping on Monday or Wednesday and boycott stores on Tuesday, September 21. This would "buy them time" to write their congresspeople and participate in peace-related activities. Although our members gladly participated, there was no visible sign of a boycott on that Tuesday.

She also spearheaded a "no war toys" campaign in local toy stores asking them to remove all war toys from the shelves for the Christmas season. We met with moderate success at local discount stores in which the managers at least talked with us. None, as far as we know, pulled their war toys.

Jean and her husband, Dan, had been active in the peace movement in California since 1963. In 1968, Dan, a Lutheran minister had joined the faculty at the Lutheran seminary on Wittenberg's campus in Springfield. Jean lost no time in becoming active with the local campus peace group. However, when the campus peace organization slowed down after the 1970 summer break, Jean turned to Springfield People for Peace.

Charles Chatfield, Wittenberg professor and a leading historian on peace movements and co-author of *An American Ordeal: The Antiwar Movement of the Vietnam Era*, said in the spring 2001 issue of *Wittenberg Magazine*, "At Wittenberg, as for many other campuses, it was as though the war had ended in the summer of 1970. Troops were coming home, and there was a general sense that the war was winding down, if slowly." This was not the sense for us.

Jean brought all kinds of new challenges to us as a group. She said her life was like a braid with three strands. One strand of war and peace, one of racial justice, and one of the women's movement. To our chagrin, she tangled all of us into her braids by her intelligent, caring, and humorous nature. To be around Jean is to be educated gently.

Unlike me, when she had a chance to hear Martin Luther King in Los Angeles back in the early 1960s, she went. King spoke at a massive outdoor event, and she remembered the radiant sunlight that struck her as so appropriate to his message. He preached the power of nonviolence and spoke in ways that made the Bible take on a new and personal meaning for Jean. A modern-day prophet, King had a radical vision, biblical in nature. His message never dimmed in her heart or in her life. She had the same effect on us.

It was at Jean and Dan's house that our kids experienced their most memorable Thanksgiving dinner—rice, tea and water! It was Jean's idea. Half a dozen Springfield People for Peace families gave up the traditional turkey and dressing and donated the money we saved to the American Friends Service Committee.

Thanksgiving afternoon, Dan led us in an ecumenical Eucharist with our children gathered around. We broke a loaf of bread and shared a cup of wine. My Catholicism kicked in, and I felt a bit disconcerted that our eight-year-old son, Mark, would be receiving communion here before he made his First Holy Communion in our church. It was a beautiful prayerful time and united us spiritually in a way we hadn't experienced before. Of course, to this day everyone's kids joke about it and act as though they had been abused that Thanksgiving. I'm sure our grandchildren will hear exaggerated stories about how rough their parents had it that Thanksgiving.

* * * * *

Two years earlier, November 10, 1969, the Springfield City Commission unanimously passed a resolution sending a message to President Nixon, both senators from Ohio and Congressman Brown. It read:

> *This Commission wants to be recorded as supporting this nation's government in its negotiations with the North Vietnamese government. The communication is further to note that, although those persons who participate in public demonstrations which seem to urge precipitous retreat from the nation's present position and obligations are within their legal rights, we consider this action to have the net effect of giving aid and comfort to the enemy, and for that reason we deplore their actions.*

In its coverage of the commission meeting and Dr. Summers' motion, the newspaper noted that the Clerk of Commission Wilma Stewart told Dr. Summers after the meeting, "In my fourteen years as a clerk, I've never had to do a harder thing than this. I don't agree with it."

Two years after the resolution passed, armed with the caravan's July survey, Ruth, Karen and Todd Liming (Treesa's son and Wittenberg student) attended the city commission meeting on October 26, 1971. Because the survey indicated 86 percent of those polled favored withdrawal of troops and 73 per cent said withdrawal should be accomplished within the next year, it seemed reasonable to ask the commission to adopt a new resolution reflecting the change of attitude of a majority of Springfield citizens. After a lengthy and emotional debate, the commission voted to postpone action for two weeks. Ruth describes her feelings then:

> *"I felt as though I was speaking to a group of aliens who had no comprehension of the language I was speaking. At times I could feel the distrust toward me, a lily-livered foolish woman who dared to express anti-government sentiment and to question our city government officials, one of whom, incidently, was a member of my church and frequently served me Communion."*

Ruth returned to the commission two weeks later and valiantly stated our case, but to no avail. The commission decided they couldn't "undo what had been done previously" and unanimously voted on a motion that "this Body not take a stand on any national policy unless it has a direct bearing on the work of the City Government." The commissioners suggested we write letters to Congressman Brown.

The city commission wasn't our only source of frustration. For many of us, our faith was at the heart of our witness, yet we found little support in our own churches. In fact, I found hostility, anger, and condemnation from my pastor.

The nun in charge of my parish CCD religion program was delighted when I answered the call for volunteer teachers because I was an experienced teacher. No longer was I just reading the book as instructed that first year in Yellow Springs! Less than a week after volunteering, I got a call from the sister. She was most embarrassed and apologetic but had no choice. The pastor, Monsignor Coleman, refused to allow me to teach because of my peace activities.

The following Sunday in his sermon at Mass, Monsignor Coleman questioned the "true" meaning of the peace symbol and lambasted war protesters as communist dupes, including those leaders in the local movement. I felt my face burn and fought back the sting of sadness and anger. I sat in my pew and debated getting up and walking out. Instead, I prayed. Not even a priest was going to intimidate me.

A few Sundays later, at morning Mass, Fr. Gavin preached that peace people were wrong because they didn't look to God for the answer. How little did he know! For years there had never been any mention of the morality of the war during Mass, no direction for the Christian conscience which must apply Christ's teachings of love to the reality of napalm, no help in applying Christ's instruction to turn the other cheek to the reality of "protective reaction" bombing. My own church broke its silence with this uncaring diatribe.

Dorothy and Arthur had a worse experience in their Methodist church. Even before they joined Springfield People for Peace, Arthur actively sought opportunities for Dorothy to speak in local churches in rural Champaign County about the war, not from the pulpit, but in the evening or for a special meeting. No surprise, no one invited her. But then because of their outspokenness about the war, one of the "leading lights" of their own church in St. Paris asked Arthur, the sweetest and most loyal patriot who ever lived, "Would you find another church?" The message was clear. They were not welcome in their own church anymore. They were disheartened. They loved teaching their Sunday school classes and for a fleeting moment hoped someone would come to their defense. It didn't happen.

Dorothy pointed out the irony of all this. Their minister, who was such a hawk during Vietnam, had been a conscientious objector during World War II. Even harder to swallow, he encouraged his own son to go into the ministry so he wouldn't be drafted. Dorothy and Arthur's son served as a combat fighter in Vietnam, and they were being accused of unpatriotic sentiment by their fellow Christians. They never joined another church.

Ruth's worst fears were confirmed when her son was wounded in combat. She and her husband were away on a trip when the telegram arrived. Upon their return, their next-door neighbor met them with telegram in hand. Ruth recalled the event:

> *"We opened it with shaking hands expecting the very worst. There was some relief in reading that Guy was wounded rather than killed, but it told us little more than that.*
> *It was several days before we learned more. Guy actually called us to reassure us that he was okay. He had been wounded in the back and leg with shrapnel and had been through surgery. He'd require at least a month to recuperate and then most likely return to combat. He still had another six months to serve. If my prayers were answered, it was at that moment—all, that is but the "return to combat" part. However, I consoled myself into believing that Guy, being a medic, might save many more lives and give other young soldiers a second chance to survive this death trap of horror."*

Ruth's frustration with the church during this period almost drove her away.

> *"As a rather typical Catholic family, we relied on the church to guide us toward an exemplary Christian lifestyle. With the war raging at its worst and many sons and daughters were dying or inflicted with physical and psychological damage, I naively expected the church to condemn the government for engaging in such an insane and obviously immoral endeavor.*
> *I desperately needed words of consolation from my Catholic friends for what my family was suffering. When Guy was wounded, I waited for the priest to offer prayers of consolation from the pulpit or at least to extend a gesture of sympathy personally to our family. No words or gestures were forthcoming, not from priests, not even from friends. And not one thank you was extended to us for sacrificing our child while theirs were safe at home, and they could sleep at night without relentlessly frightening nightmares. The only words of sympathy and consolation came from*

other members of the peace movement. They knew, they understood. They were not afraid to speak the truth."

Dan Martensen tried to get the board of the *Lutheran Quarterly* to devote just one issue to the Vietnam War but they refused. We all agreed with him when he said, "Most ministers hope the war will go away and their congregations won't get into tense discussions over it." Blessed are the peacemakers!

Chapter Thirteen

Peace to Politics

1972—Nixon visits China and Russia as North Vietnam opens a major offensive in the south. The United States responds with massive bombings in the south as well as in the north, including Hanoi. The last U.S. combat unit is withdrawn in August, leaving 44,000 American military personnel in South Vietnam.

Between Dorothy and Vern and the emerging 1972 elections, we became more aware of the need for political clout. We needed those in office who believed as we did. It didn't matter how many minds we could change—unless those minds were the ones making the decisions in Washington.

Nixon would be running for re-election. Hubert Humphrey, Johnson's former vice president, would probably win the Democratic nomination, but those of us in the peace movement didn't trust him. The old ties were too strong for us. He was too linked to Johnson and the war. McCarthy or McGovern: We trusted them, but could they win against Nixon?

On the local front, Congressman Clarence J. Brown, Jr., was running unopposed. Brown virtually inherited the office from his father in 1965 after C. J. Brown, Sr.'s, twenty-four years as congressman. Brown, Jr., was so entrenched no Democrat would take him on.

At our first Springfield People for Peace meeting of 1972, Dorothy bemoaned the fact that Brown would run unopposed in the general election. My husband Jim happened to be at that meeting. In his usual style of pushing me out the door, he challenged Dorothy to run. Dorothy kept shaking her head no, but Jim and Arthur both nodded yes, and we all knew Dorothy would run.

Dorothy, a fifty-four year old grandmother of two, farmer's wife, and high school graduate, entered the congressional race as an Independent on January 17, 1972.

At the same meeting that gave birth to Dorothy's campaign, Vern asked Karen and me to meet with him later to talk about the presidential election. I asked Jean Martensen (who coordinated the "no buy" movement) to join us because, as I perceived, she had some savvy about the political scene. I knew nothing of politics, nor did Karen. Vern, Karen, Jean, and I sat on the floor of her faculty apartment on Wittenberg's campus. Vern, who seemed to me to be a walking encyclopedia on history and politics, gave us a short course on the process of electing delegates to the national convention as well as a pep talk on why McGovern was our man, as opposed to McCarthy. Vern pointed out McGovern had co-sponsored the McGovern Hatfield Amendment to end the war back in 1970 (the one Ruth and I lobbied for in Washington) and McCarthy didn't do anything. That settled that!

Earlier in 1969, McGovern was appointed to chair a commission to ensure fairness in selecting delegates to the Democrat convention. Under his leadership, the entire electoral system had been opened up. Delegates were to be elected in the year of the convention to ensure they reflected the voters' current wishes. Women, youth, and minorities were to be adequately represented. This presented an opportunity unprecedented in this country.

Vern knew the local Democrat party leaders were supporting Humphrey. None of them supported McGovern, and as such no one did the leg work to get him on the ballot for the May primary. If we didn't take on this task, no one would have the opportunity to vote for him, including us. Even if it were seen as a token vote, it was important to us. We wanted to make a statement about the war, and we knew others would too. People deserved the choice to vote for a peace candidate. By the end of the evening, we agreed to do whatever it took to get McGovern's name on the ballot for the seventh Congressional District.

We organized the caucus for McGovern which, by law, had to be open to the public. We passed the necessary paperwork to the state party, placed the legal ads announcing the caucus in the paper, lined up people who would like to run as delegates, reserved a room for the election of delegates at our caucus, and in general did everything we were told to do by the McGovern people, staffers from D.C. Needless to say, they were delighted we had surfaced. The deadline for the entire process was only days away, but we pulled it off. (McCarthy's campaign failed to materialize in our congressional district, and his name did not appear on the primary ballot.)

The McGovern caucus was held at the Scot's Inn in Springfield in early February 1972. We had a bigger turnout than expected; probably 35 voters, very respectable for this conservative district. We were to elect four delegates, all pledged to McGovern. (The number of delegates was based on the population in each congressional district.) Because of my commitment as chair of Springfield People for Peace and my experience at the Paris Peace Talks, I won nomination as a delegate along with three others.

The other three delegates were not members of Springfield People for Peace. In fact, I didn't know any of them. Jim Mitchell was a Vietnam veteran, an employee of International Harvester (now Navistar), a UAW-CAP council representative and active in the Young Democrats. A black woman, Jewel Graham, director of the social work program at Antioch College and assistant professor of social welfare, originally supported Congresswoman Shirley Chisholm for president (the first black woman to run for president). Robert Turoff, associate professor of physics at Antioch College, was a newcomer to politics. We were strangers, but not for long.

In Ohio the delegates pledged to their presidential candidate were elected in each congressional district as one slate of delegates. Jim, Jewel, Robert, and I would win or lose together. First, we needed to get our petitions signed and filed with the board of elections. The rules and regulations were drummed into us by the McGovern staff. We heard horror story after horror story of petitions being thrown out due to technicalities.

Once we jumped the petition hurdle for McGovern, we still had to get 6,000 valid voter signatures (Democrat, Republic, or Independent) by March to get Dorothy's name on the ballot in November. Bundled up against the snow, we carried her petitions in Champaign's county seat Urbana, stopping people on the street and asking for their signatures. Surely it was the most aggressive campaign ever seen there. For weeks, we hit bowling alleys, cafes, and busy intersections all over the district trying to convince people to vote for a peace candidate. It took eight weeks to gather well over 6,000 signatures. We held our breath as we waited to hear if the petitions were accepted. They were. Dorothy's name would be on the ballot in the general election in November 1972.

That spring, we set up McGovern headquarters in downtown Springfield. The place was always hopping, volunteers addressing envelopes, people on phone banks, and literature and yard signs counted and readied for distribution. I'd even stop in after work at 11:30 P.M. to connect with people still there. One night I pulled my car to the curb around the corner from headquarters. Just as I was turning the ignition off, a man got in the car on the passenger side. He looked like a "Mr. Milquetoast." This time (as compared to the incident in Yellow Springs) I jumped out of the car and yelled, "What are you doing?" He looked shocked and embarrassed and hurriedly got out and ran away. I told the guys in headquarters what happened, and they roared with laughter. I had parked in a pick-up area for hookers. Poor soul thought I was his.

The Seventh Congressional District in Ohio is a very conservative rural district. McGovern, portrayed as ultra-liberal, didn't have a chance. One of the cardinal rules for politics is to believe you can win. I didn't—not here in our district—but I believed in McGovern, and I was willing to work.

We managed to get two young McGovern staffers assigned here to help our local campaign. The Humphrey delegates and party people never thought that a grassroots McGovern push here could actually make a difference. In fact, there never was a campaign like it locally. We rounded up hundreds of volunteers. The excitement, passion, and purpose overrode all negative thoughts. Even if we didn't win, we were getting our message out. If elected, McGovern would end the war.

Karen and I pulled our little ones in a wagon while the older kids went door to door handing out campaign literature. It became a way of life. Telephone banks were set up in headquarters and constantly manned. We each took our turns at the phones, a job none of us liked but endured. Phone banks were set up in Jean's musty, block-walled, concrete floor basement. For weeks, dozens of Wittenberg students filed in day and evening to help with the calls. The craziness went on until the May primary.

Primary election day came. Our district had never seen such a drive to get out the vote. The night prior to Election Day, hundreds of volunteers papered targeted neighborhoods with leaflets throughout the seven counties making up our congressional district. People would wake up—on Election Day—and see that someone believed enough in McGovern to come to their home during the night to win their vote. It was a mission!

Late that election night, results showed Humphrey the winner. We were disappointed, but knew the odds had been incredibly against us. We could still hope for a McGovern win when it really counted, at the Democratic National Convention and finally election night in November. Cock-eyed optimists!

I went to bed that night, tossed and turned, and prayed. Late the following morning, after the Humphrey delegates celebrated at a breakfast, I got a phone call from Jim Mitchell. There were late votes counted and some mix-up and Humphrey didn't win. McGovern won! We won!

Besides all the wonder of our political system and the hope for McGovern as president, I couldn't believe that I, Peggy Hanna, was going to Miami, Florida, as a delegate to a national convention. I remembered watching television with my dad during the 1954 Republican National Convention. I was only in the seventh grade but curious about how all those people got to go there. He explained they were politicians and workers within the party. After many years of service, a lucky few were rewarded by getting to go to the convention. Hardly anyone got to be a delegate, just the big shots.

Delegates were and still are responsible for their own expenses for the convention. A fund raiser, a house party, was held in Yellow Springs to help us with some of the cost. Outside of an orientation meeting for delegates, things were a bit slower for us between the May primary and the July convention. Jim and I decided he would fly with me to Florida and hope he could get a visitor's pass into the convention hall for at least one day. We'd farm the kids out to family and friends. It'd be a week together we'd never forget.

Actually we'd never forget the beginning of that week, before we even got to the convention.

My sister and her family in West Chicago, Illinois, volunteered to watch our two oldest boys. Our dear friends, Mike and Judy, in Griffith, Indiana, took the three younger kids. After dropping the kids off at the respective homes, Jim and I boarded our plane at Chicago's O'Hare Airport. With seat belts fastened and the engines roaring for take off, a stewardess suddenly approached us in our seats. "Mr. and Mrs. Hanna, there's an emergency phone call for you." Dumbfounded, Jim and I glanced at each other as she added, "We can hold the plane for you for a few minutes. Follow me."

We rushed through the plane into the terminal where they led us to a phone. I grabbed the phone, not giving Jim a chance to get it. Judy was on the line, crying over and over, "I'm so sorry, I'm so sorry."

"What's wrong? What's happened?" I asked but she kept repeating, "I'm so sorry."
I shouted at her, "Is somebody dead?"
And the answer I needed came. "No."
There was hope for whatever we were facing. Judy then calmed down and explained, in a voice choking with tears and fear, that seven-year-old Kevin was in intensive care in a hospital in Hammond, Indiana. He had fallen off his bike, hit his head, and had a severe concussion, and was still unconscious. Jim and I ran for a cab and rushed to borrow a car from my parents who lived about forty minutes from the airport. We both prayed and supported each other as best we could during the two-hour drive to the hospital. Fear engulfed us as we drove with no contact with the hospital or Mike and Judy. Kevin remained unconscious all night. He lay in a crib in the center of an adult intensive care unit. There was no pediatric intensive care unit, just a huge open room with dozens of beds, patients of all ages, and machines and tubes everywhere.

The next morning he finally came to. He awoke in that metal crib, which looked more like a cage than a bed, looked at his nurse, and asked, "Am I in jail?"

Kevin was well, and the next day I flew to Miami just in time for the opening of the convention. Jim would join me a couple days later. Of course, our luggage flew on without us. When I finally did catch up to it at the motel, the lock had jammed, and I couldn't get it open. I was still in my slacks and shirt from the past two days. Desperate, I finally found a maintenance man who opened the lock. I rushed to shower and dress for the big event. I was so nervous; my hands trembled while I tried putting on my makeup. I had no idea where any of the other delegates were. I'm not sure when I had ever felt so alone. This was right up there with hailing a cab in Paris. At least this time, I was able to telephone for a taxi and headed to the convention hall.

Remembering what conventions looked like on TV—delegates sleeping, eating, and talking instead of listening to the speakers addressing them—I resolved to pay attention and do my job conscientiously. So, as usual, I was one of a very few who listened intently and spent my time doing what I believed was the serious work of being a delegate.

The only thing that worried me as a delegate was my being pressured or lobbied to desert McGovern or any of the platform. My dad had told me how Humphrey people might try to win me over to their side, but it didn't happen. No one approached me for anything! I felt pretty nonexistent.

It was truly exciting though to see all the senators I'd seen on TV and newscasters like Walter Cronkite. Crowds clogged the aisles and camera operators and newscasters pressed through to get interviews. Once I saw Roger Mudd almost get into a fist fight while climbing over people to get to someone. Once I found myself standing in a clump of people surrounding Jesse Jackson, dressed in brightly colored African garb, and Congresswoman Bella Abzug under her huge trademark hat. I had a short conversation with women's rights activist and founder of *Ms.* Magazine, Gloria Steinem, as we, without choice, squooshed through a crowd together.

Ohio had a split delegation, the majority being Humphrey delegates and led by AFL-CIO union leader, Frank King. King detested the McGovern "peaceniks" who had no business being delegates. The Humphrey delegates openly harassed us, but we never took the bait. They were older, more mature, and dressed in suits, but we, young, inexperienced, and a bit casual in our dress, took the high road and didn't succumb to swearing back at them.

They did do us in though on the evening of the actual election of the presidential nominee. Because they had the majority, Frank King was elected as the chair of our Ohio delegation. As such, every day he received all the delegates' credentials for entry into the convention. On Thursday, election night, he didn't distribute the credentials to us McGovern delegates.

Some of the McGovern leaders cautioned us to bide our time. He's just playing with us they said, but by the time we were to board the buses to the convention hall, we still didn't have our credentials. We boarded the buses around 5 P.M., believing they'd soon be bringing the credentials. We'd just wait it out.

The temperature outside had to have been well into the 90s. By 6 o'clock, someone boarded the bus, not with our credentials, but with Kentucky Fried Chicken (donated by Colonel Sanders, who later came by to say hello). As we sweltered in the heat and ate chicken, licked our fingers (they forgot napkins), and our "wounds," we decided to go on to the convention hall with the expectation the credentials would be waiting for us there.

However, without the credentials, we didn't get past the parking lot guard. Tempers began to get hot as we were held hostage to Frank King's treachery. Some suggested we just storm into the convention. The time past for the convention to convene, we imagined the press questioning what happened to the rest of the Ohio delegation. Boy, we'd tell them! We'd make Frank King pay! It'd been well over three hours since we boarded the bus. Finally someone approached our bus, and we got our credentials. We marched into the hall just minutes prior to the vote. We expected all kinds of attention and questions as to what had happened. We'd tell them! However, none of the press was even aware; no one missed us or cared. King won his game.

But then again, we won the convention. That night McGovern won the nomination, and most of his platform remained intact. We were delirious. We never dreamed we'd get this far. Now if we could get him elected president, we would end the war.

Chapter Fourteen

Political Realities

1972—Jane Fonda goes to Hanoi. Congress passes the Equal Rights Amendment. Nixon wins re-election. The Paris Peace Talks resume after a lengthy disruption. Nixon initiates the "Christmas Bombings" of North Vietnam until December 31 when negotiations are resumed.

All 1972 Springfield People for Peace activities focused on the two political campaigns, first for the primary for McGovern and then the general election for McGovern and Dorothy Franke. Dorothy's husband served as her campaign manager and chief cheerleader. His respect for and confidence in her bordered on the obsessive. He set up speaking engagements; hammered out yard signs and hunted destinations for them; designed her literature; walked door to door with her; chauffeured her everywhere to parades, perch dinners, pancake breakfasts, and anywhere they could find a soap box. The only thing he didn't do was raise money. He'd rather spend his own than ask for donations. They covered their campaign expenses, primarily gas money which was significant since the district encompassed seven counties. The campaign consumed Dorothy and Arthur.

Dorothy's trademark was her hat. All her adult life, she had always worn one, so Arthur capitalized on this idiosyncrasy by mounting a huge flowered straw hat (inverted laundry basket complete with rim and flowers) on the top of her bottom-of-the-line Chevy. A picture of her and the car made the front page of the Springfield paper. However, Dorothy's campaign wasn't just gimmick; people compared her to Will Rogers. In fact, since 1957 she'd been writing a weekly humor column for the *Urbana Daily Citizen* whose publisher was the very same Congressman Clarence J. Brown, Jr. With her homespun wit and sharp intellect, she campaigned on issues beyond ending the war, issues ahead of her time: term limitations for senators and representatives, a statewide high-speed rail system, protecting the family farm, and revenue sharing for local communities.

Of course, with no money for a "real" campaign, Dorothy remained virtually unknown because of the scope and size of the district and the name she was running against. To make matters even more difficult, some parades and community suppers open to the incumbent Congressman Brown blocked Dorothy's participation by saying "candidates not allowed," though office holders were welcomed! However we all saw her campaign as a process, an opportunity to educate for change. No matter what, it'd all be worth it.

After the convention in July, volunteers and staffers from the national campaign moved into our McGovern headquarters. We continued working as before the primary with our hearts and souls poured into it. We never lost focus on why we so desperately needed McGovern to win. Ours was a mission of peace, not politics for politics' sake.

As part of our campaign for both McGovern and Dorothy, I'd call in to the Smilin' Bob show on behalf of my candidates. That same summer, actress Jane Fonda flew to Hanoi, and the entire country was in an uproar over her pictures with the North Vietnamese and her radio broadcasts. Although a part of me could admire her for standing up for what she believed in, I hated that she had gone over the edge; in fact, did harm to both our forces and to the peace movement itself. (Ironically while writing this book, I happened to see her being interviewed by Barbara Walters on the TV show *20/20*. Jane said, "It just kills me that I did things that hurt those men. It was never my intention.")

Sometime after her trip, Smilin' Bob, while on the air, either in ignorance or with malice, dubbed *me* as "Hanoi Hanna." He never once addressed me that way, only when I wasn't on the air. I chose to ignore it and pretend I didn't know. I had worked so hard to be a credible person in my work as a peace activist and campaign worker and felt angry, embarrassed, and denigrated. Even today some people jokingly refer to me with that name. I don't think it's funny.

Election night that November started out with a cautious but hopeful air. Ironically, the very first election results to come over the radio had Dorothy leading Brown by a significant number. Still at home getting ready for the election night party, I ran to turn the news up louder and crashed my little toe into the leg of the stereo. My first and only broken bone. A few minutes later the announcer came on and corrected himself. He had reversed the numbers.

Early returns projected a big loss for McGovern and for Dorothy. It was as if there had been a death in the family. There was no bringing them back, it was final. People cried and barely spoke. We had all worked so hard and believed strongly in each of them.

Dorothy remained philosophical about her loss and hurt more for us than for herself. We hurt for her and Arthur and for our district's loss.

McGovern's loss was devastating. Feelings of disappointment, anger, fear, and frustration, multiplied by my sympathy for my friends who worked so hard and for the people who would still suffer unnecessarily under a prolonged war, bordered on making me ill.

We, Springfield People for Peace, never really regained our strength. The holidays were coming, and we assured ourselves that we deserved and needed a break. We'd regroup after New Year's, January 1973.

While we tried to celebrate the Prince of Peace's birthday, the season of peace, Nixon initiated the massive Christmas Bombings, the heaviest aerial bombardment of North Vietnam of the entire war, bombings that killed 2,200 civilians.

Chapter Fifteen

The End

1973—The Paris Peace Accords are signed. Military draft ends. U.S. troops are withdrawn, although U.S. military commitment to the South Vietnamese government extends through the continuing war until Hanoi's final, successful offensive in the spring of 1975.

Total Dead

Americans (including MIAs)	58,202	American Allies Korea	4,407
South Vietnam	220,357	Australia/	
North Vietnam/Vietcong	851,000	New Zealand	469
		Thailand	352

Millions of civilians killed.

Like the peace movement throughout the country, Springfield People for Peace lost its momentum with Nixon's election. Our service personnel were coming home. Not as we wanted—the war wasn't over—but they were coming home. We met once in January 1973. Ruth and I, like Treesa before us, told the group we wanted to step down as co-chairs. I personally was exhausted, and so was my family. My tour of duty was over.

Over the years and in different ways, some more than others, peace people paid a price for standing up against the war. We paid in fractured relationships. All of us in the peace movement have stories of upset families, co-workers, friends, and neighbors. Ruth's family simply dismissed her and never talked about it although she wanted and needed to talk about it, as we all did. Karen's father, a vocal hawk, angrily accused her of being a communist dupe. The war became a forbidden subject, even with her sisters and mother. My family, even though many of them opposed the war, treated me like nothing had ever happened with a major part of my life. Nothing said, nothing asked. For years, my older brother didn't speak to me. Like the nurse whose son was at Kent State, he, too, said my kids would someday blow up buildings.

As I write this thirty years later, I do take some comfort in knowing we were right. I wasn't a communist dupe! But it's little comfort, too many wounds are still not healed. The peace movement's role during Vietnam is a subject that's buried, but not gone. Although most people, even veterans, have come to believe the war was a mistake, many still see the peace movement as unpatriotic. Translate that to they see "peace people" as unpatriotic, even to blame for losing the war. No mean words spoken, but the silent response and the quick change of subject says a lot when my peace past is mentioned. I get the message.

I think the image most damning of the peace movement (or war protesters) isn't one of burning buildings or even the flag, but the image of antiwar activists spitting on our soldiers when they came home. There's denial on the part of many peace people that this ever really happened, because it's beyond comprehension. But now, yes, I think there were some such incidents, but to paint all peace activists with the same brush would be like painting all soldiers with the brush of My Lai. There's truth to be sure on both sides that people did unspeakable things, hateful acts against others. But what good is it to concentrate only on the worst of both sides? All of us know in our own heart and conscience whether we need forgiveness or to forgive. Sometimes, maybe it's both.

If I had to do it all over again, there's only one thing I'd change. I have heard people criticize us as though it was our fault there was no celebration for the soldiers coming home. Of course, this ignores the fact that those in the peace movement were a minority and begs the question, where were the majority of Americans? Why didn't *they* organize parades and celebrations to honor our men and women returning from Vietnam? Of course, our vets need much more than parades, but they didn't even get that.

Therefore, the one thing I'd change would have been to use the peace movement as a catalyst to welcome our vets home. No one else did, maybe we could have.

I love my country—unconditionally, as a mother loves her child. However, it's not a blind love; I see her faults, know her sins. Just as parents help shape their children, I believe we as citizens must recognize our responsibility in shaping our country's values and policies. This is what democracy demands. We honor those who fought for our freedom by utilizing that freedom, by exercising those very rights for which they put their lives on the line.

It's painful to think of all the lives lost or haunted for a war that shouldn't have been fought, that couldn't have been won. Even so, nothing can diminish the sacrifices and bravery of so many who did what their country asked them to do. Maybe in some ways the pain of Vietnam is a positive pain. A pain that will always remind us, we must do everything in our power to work for peace without sacrificing our sons and daughters.

In 1986 I had an opportunity to meet with a group of Vietnam veterans who shared their stories and anger with me. I had run (unsuccessfully) for state representative, an outgrowth of becoming politically active during Vietnam. During the campaign, the incumbent state representative called a press conference with the local Vietnam vets group in front of the war memorial in Bellefontaine, Ohio. He labeled me a traitor because of my peace activism during Vietnam. The reporter called me at home and asked if I'd like to speak to the vets before he wrote his story. It was a forty-five minute drive, but they were willing to wait for me.

No time to change out of my blue jeans (to keep up the image of "the candidate") or to think of what I might be facing, I drove the back roads north to Bellefontaine. I found the address; an old dilapidated building with a forbidding-looking entrance on an alley. About a dozen Vietnam vets dressed in jeans and T-shirts sat or stood in a semi-circle filling the small room where we met. I felt shaky but determined that my nervousness and fear would not paralyze me. The reporter asked me to tell my story.

I told them much of what I've written here. I didn't know if they'd believe me or if what I said would make any difference to them, or even if they'd attack me—verbally, of course, not physically. But as I spoke, their reactions dumbfounded me. They were shocked. They were angry, but not with me! They had believed the stories fed to them by their commanding officers, stories about those commie-loving traitorous demonstrators. They knew only what they saw in the media back at home. They thought people like me hated them. I was shocked to realize they never had a chance to know what we *assumed* they knew—how much we truly cared about them and how driven we were to bring them home. I had no idea how the images of violence on the part of a minority of protesters, as portrayed in the news, skewed the message we carried in our hearts.

In church terms, it was a time of reconciliation. A sense of acceptance and understanding replaced the tension and anger present when I first entered the room an hour and half earlier. Every one of them shook my hand and warmly thanked me as they left. Not only did they believe me, but all pledged their support for my candidacy (except one older vet who shook my hand but did not say those magic words, "You've got my vote").

Feeling enormous relief that they believed me, that they understood, I drove home in tears. I thought about how Vietnam veterans and peace people needed to come together like this all over the country, to understand, to forgive, and to heal.

That was over fifteen years ago. Will it, can it ever happen?

* * * * *

September 11, 2001, hurt the heart and soul of our country. Patriotism salved our pain and united us in expressing our fear and profound grief. My local elementary school held a patriotic program shortly after 9/11. Little primary grade children, dressed in red, white, and blue, sang their hearts out about love of our country. Local veterans were introduced and honored for their contributions during the last several wars. I could barely contain myself from dissolving into a puddle of tears.

Eventually, however, tears gave way to apprehension with the war in Afghanistan and then to anger as our country rushed to war in Iraq.

As I listened, learned, and joined in the debate about the wisdom and morality of going to war in Iraq, the differences of opinion expressed by those for and against the war, while passionate, were respectful. It wasn't until the war itself that those of us in opposition to the war were once again branded as unpatriotic. Worse, we were told we didn't support our troops!

It feels trite to have to say that peace activists do support our men and women in uniform. We want them safe and home with their families. We respect them for their sacrifices. We understand that the freedom to dissent publicly was won for us by those who laid their lives on the line. We share these common convictions with all Americans. At the same time, peace people must not be silenced or intimidated by the twisting of our opposition to the war in Iraq, or any war, to the false message of not supporting our troops.

Peace activists are strong individuals representing a broad spectrum of beliefs, but we share common concerns about war, about specific wars, history, and morality. We know the arguments about how peace demonstrations aid the enemy and prolong war, arguments espoused by the government in an effort to repress opposition. We understand the animosity toward us, but without public dissent, our government could interpret such silence as license to pursue a policy of might makes right. Without us, what are the checks and balances on unrestrained power? It's because we love our country and those protecting it that we are willing to stand up and speak out.

The lessons of Vietnam must never be ignored or forgotten. We are no longer innocents who unquestioningly believe everything told to us. Vietnam taught us that. We can never again sacrifice our sons and daughters to political rhetoric and unsubstantiated fears. We, the people, must question, challenge, and act. It's the only way a true democracy can survive.

APPENDIX

Brief Overview of the Events Leading to the Vietnam War

In 1858, the French occupied Vietnam. During France's entire rule, there were constant peasant uprisings but to no avail. In 1930 and 1931 thousands of Vietnamese were executed and imprisoned by the French Legion in an attempt to suppress all nationalist parties. A young man named Ngo Dinh Diem assisted the French during this time and would later be chosen by the United States to be president of South Vietnam.

Japan, with no resistance from the French, occupied Vietnam in 1940. During the 1940 to 1945 period, all Vietnamese groups struggling for independence from the French and the Japanese formed a coalition under the leadership of Ho Chi Minh. They called themselves the League for Independence or the Vietminh.

On September 2, 1945, the day Japan surrendered to the Allies, Ho Chi Minh announced the formation of the Democratic Republic of Vietnam and read to the crowds in Hanoi the Vietnamese "Declaration of Independence." At that time, the new republic included all of Vietnam. Three weeks later, the British were helping to re-establish French rule and forced the Vietminh out of Saigon. During this time, Ho Chi Minh tried to gain support from President Truman but received none.

By 1947, French troops occupied Hanoi and the fight for independence was on again. In early 1950, the French brought in the former Vietnamese emperor, Bao Dai, to serve as president, thus the United States could recognize

Bao Dai (the French puppet government) and help the French without appearing to bolster colonialism. By 1954, 250,000 Frenchmen were fighting in Vietnam and the United States was financing most of the cost of the war. Finally in the spring of 1954, the Vietnamese defeated the French at Dien Bien Phu.

The warring parties, including the United States, France, China, Great Britain, Laos, Cambodia, the Democratic Republic of Vietnam (Ho Chi Minh and the Vietminh) and the "State" of Vietnam (Bao Dai), attempted to settle the political problems following the end of French colonial rule. Even though the Democratic Republic of Vietnam controlled over three-fourths of Vietnam ground, they agreed to a temporary administrative separation of north and south Vietnam at the seventeenth parallel. This was never to be seen as a permanent division.

It was also agreed that elections would be held within two years to unify the country. Neither zone would receive help or enter into international alliances. The United States and the Bao Dai regime were the only ones not to accept the Geneva Agreements, but the United States did promise not to go against them. The United States then pressured the French to replace Bao Dai with Ngo Dinh Diem as prime minister of the Republic of Vietnam.

The Vietnamese, as a united country, were to decide for themselves in 1956 which government they preferred, but the United States knew Communist Ho Chi Minh would be elected by a landslide so they refused to allow the elections to be held. This was in violation of the Geneva Agreements that recognized Vietnam as one country and one people.

Our involvement grew while Diem's rule became a ruthless, mercenary dictatorship supposedly aimed at communists but actually brutalizing any opposition. At the same time, the American people were led to believe Diem was a dedicated, respected advocate of freedom and democracy.

By December 1960, the National Liberation Front (NLF), a resistance movement in the south, organized their armed forces (Vietcong). Within two years, the NLF controlled eighty percent of the countryside. By 1965, the United States was forced to admit defeat or widen the war in an effort for victory. President Johnson then initiated the bombing of North Vietnam and committed U.S. ground troops to South Vietnam. Victory was ever elusive.

BIBLIOGRAPHY

Vietnam in Photographs and Text. Felix Greene, Fulton Publishing Company, Palo Alto, CA, 1966.

In Retrospect, The Tragedy and Lessons of Vietnam, Robert S. McNamara with Brian VanDeMark, Times Books, Random House, New York, 1995.

Argument Without End, In Search of Answers to the Vietnam Tragedy, Robert S. McNamara, James Blight, Robert Brigham, Thomas Biersteker and Col. Herbert Schandler, Public Affairs, New York, 1999.

Our War and What It Did to Us. David Harris, Random House, New York 1996.

A Grand Delusion, America's Descent into Vietnam, Robert Mann, Basic Books, Perseus Book Group, New York, 2001.

The Tragedy of Vietnam, Patrick J. Hearden, Harper Collins Publishers, New York, 1991.

An American Ordeal, The Antiwar Movement of the Vietnam Era, Charles DeBenedetti, Charles Chatfield, Syracuse University Press, Syracuse, NY, 1990.